Editorial

Reinventing Socialism

Among all the smiles and handshakes and touching reconciliations, and in the convenient amnesia which has fostered the governing coalition in Britain, we can hear the nearly noiseless cranking up of drawbridges and steady quiet preparation for battle. Once again, it is the unions which are to provoke all this attention, and above all, the public sector unions. The Government has declared its need to draw back from a fiscal deficit of 11.1% of output. The first six billion pounds worth of cuts have already been announced. More, many more, are to follow, as an autumn spending review festers in preparation. Government employees await the next move with justified trepidation. Almost seventy per cent of them are governed by agreements on collective bargaining. All these are in the sights of the neo-liberals who now regulate our affairs.

There are many prongs to their projected offensive. Tighter pay settlements were already conveniently announced by the outgoing New Labour administration. Privatisation will contract out a larger proportion of public services to private profiteers, who customarily discover convenient ways of eroding wage settlements. Not only must collective agreements be steered into the new culture of squeeze, but national pay bargaining itself comes under attack. Our new masters wish to reform what they call rigid pay structures and agreements such as those governing working conditions in schools.

Schools are not the only places in which conditions can be eroded by the decentralisation of bargaining. If you live in a poor area, then clearly you deserve poorer wages. Does the market not decree official parsimony? If the evaluation of your work gives you low ratings, then your pay deserves to be further reduced accordingly. Once this principle is established, even if you have good ratings you will be in competition with other people who do not, and this mean market will depress your earnings, too. Cutting pay and perks is a fine economy which will commend itself to our shiny new rulers. But overtime hours are also a tempting target. If overtime can be exacted without payment, this is more tempting still. As always, in times of stress, pensions quickly demand central attention. Mayhem has already been unleashed in many sectors, but we must expect that ferocious new attacks are in preparation.

How can the coalition cohere through the battles it has already determined to promote? Readers of *The Orange Book*, published in 2004 to reclaim

Liberalism, may be less doubtful than is fashionable, on this score. *The Orange Book* was edited by David Laws MP, who, before his hapless descent into politics, had been Vice President at J. P. Morgan and Company, and then Managing Director at Barclays De Zoete Wedd before becoming Director of Policy for the Liberal Democrats between 1997 and 1999. It may be that he was not altogether uncomfortable in his new role as axe man while it lasted. At least he never got to play it alongside Peter Mandelson, which fact may have terminated yet another undesirable career and example.

David Laws announced his reclaiming agenda by enunciating three principles which govern Liberalism. These began with freedom from all forms of oppression, and included oppression by the State, the tyranny of majorities, as well as ignorance, intolerance, prejudice and conformity. They did not include freedoms which might impinge upon the interests of the proprietors of big industries or commerce. The second key element of Liberalism was the belief that power should be exercised through accountable and democratic structures as close to the people as possible. These structures also did not include those of big companies, which might very well be improved by strong tests of democratic accountability. Would it not be nice to subject their Chief Executives to due processes of popular election and recall? But these might undermine the third strand of Liberalism

> 'which is the belief in the value of free trade, open competition, market mechanisms, consumer power, and the effectiveness of the private sector. These beliefs are combined with opposition to monopolies and instinctive suspicion of State control and interference particularly in relationship to the ownership and control of business.'

True, Laws sees as an essential element of Liberalism, a fourth principle: Social Liberalism, as embodied in the instruments of welfare handed down to us by Lloyd George.

But the sovereignty of the market did not bring about the old age pension, which owes more to the admittedly feeble sovereignty of the electorate, and would, if allowed so to do, be likely to annul market dominance in short order. The sovereignty of the market has also proved an extremely insufficient guarantee of housing standards for poorer people. Indeed, market sovereignty itself has, during the recent economic crisis, done much to undermine the institution of markets. David Laws, it is true, is not now in a pole position to sort all that out. Whether his chosen substitute is up to the task remains to be seen.

It had fallen to the Orange champion to present the detailed schedule of the government's project to slice that £6.2 billion out of governmental

The Spokesman
Reinventing Socialism

Edited by Ken Coates
Assistant Editor Tony Simpson

Published by Spokesman for the
Bertrand Russell Peace Foundation

Spokesman 109   2010

CONTENTS

Editorial
Reinventing Socialism   3   *Ken Coates*

Clause IV   15   *Sidney Webb*

'We cannot administer capitalism'   19   *Clement Attlee*

Blair's Initiative   24   *Ken Coates*

*   *   *

Ken Coates – A Tribute

A Flower of the Labour Movement   31

*   *   *

The Radical Intellectual   43   *Noam Chomsky*

'Maybe we should talk about my books'   57   *Henning Mankell*

What the Spooks Want   59   *Tony Simpson*

David Kelly: A fresh inquiry?   65

Why I am a Guildsman   67   *Bertrand Russell*

Reviews   70   *Ken Coates, Abi Rhodes, Bruce Kent, Stan Newens, Tony Simpson, Michael Barratt Brown, Richard Minns, John Daniels, Henry McCubbin, Christopher Gifford*

Subscriptions
Institutions £35.00
Individuals £20.00 (UK)
           £25.00 (ex UK)

Back issues available on request

A CIP catalogue record for this book is available from the British Library

Published by the
Bertrand Russell Peace Foundation Ltd.,
Russell House
Bulwell Lane
Nottingham NG6 0BT
England
Tel. 0115 9784504
email:
elfeuro@compuserve.com
www.spokesmanbooks.com
www.russfound.org

Editorial Board:
Michael Barratt Brown
John Daniels
Ken Fleet
Stuart Holland
Tony Simpson

Mixed Sources
Product group from well-managed forests and other controlled sources

Cert no. SGS-COC-006541
www.fsc.org
© 1996 Forest Stewardship Council

ISSN 1367 7748   Printed by the Russell Press Ltd., Nottingham, UK   ISBN 978 0 85124 779 3

This number of *The Spokesman* is very much as Ken Coates shaped it. He had completed his editorial, where we found our title. There were some loose ends to tie up, and we had agreed to do that after the weekend. Then came the news of his sudden death, on Sunday 27th June. Our work was put on hold, at least for a short while, whilst tributes poured in. We have chosen a selection from these to complete the contents of this issue.

Forty years earlier, in 1970, writing the Editorial Notes for very first issue of *The Spokesman*, Ken had remarked Russell's own anticipation of the new journal during what proved to be the last week of his own life: 'He had wanted the journal desperately in order to be able, the better, to organise support in all the various battles in which he was engaged'. As Ken then said of Russell, so we may now also say of him, *The Spokesman* is dedicated to carrying on that work.

Tony Simpson

* * *

'I have always believed that true socialism will be made by the people themselves, the real beneficiaries. That was the significant achievement of the Institute for Workers' Control, because it encouraged people to work out their own ideas about what might constitute democracy in industry. This put paid to Fabian myths about how our teachers always knew best, even if that experience was short-lived.'

Ken Coates, 25 June 2010

> ## Once again we must ask: 'Who governs?'
>
> ' ... The implicit premise of the coming retrenchment is that market economies are always at, or rapidly return to, full employment. It follows that a stimulus, whether fiscal or monetary, cannot improve on the existing situation. All that increased government spending does is to withdraw money from the private sector; all that printing money does is to cause inflation.
>
> These propositions are a re-run of the famous 'Treasury view' of 1929. By contrast, Keynes argued that demand can fall short of supply, and that when this happened, government vice turned into virtue. In a slump, governments should increase, not reduce, their deficits to make up for the deficit in private spending. Any attempt by government to increase its saving (in other words, to balance its budget) would only worsen the slump. This was his "paradox of thrift". The current stampede to thrift shows that the re-conversion to Keynes in the wake of the financial collapse of 2008 was only skin-deep: the first story remains deeply lodged in the minds of economists and politicians.
>
> But this story alone does not explain the conversion to austerity. Politicians clamouring for cuts in public spending do not cite Chicago University economists. They talk about the need to restore 'confidence in the markets'. The argument here is that deficits do positive harm by destroying business confidence. This collapse of confidence may come in several forms – fear of higher taxes, fear of default, fear of inflation. Deficits thus delay the natural (and rapid) recovery of the economy. If markets have come to the view that deficits are harmful, they must be appeased, even if they are wrong. What market participants believe to be the case becomes the case, not because their beliefs are true, but because they act on their beliefs, true or false ... '
>
> Lord Skidelsky, *Financial Times*, 16 June 2010

spending. According to the *Financial Times* at least 30,000 jobs, and possibly more than 50,000, will be eliminated this year as a result.

> 'But those tens of thousands of lost jobs and frozen posts will be just a small down payment – well under 10 per cent on the massive reduction in public sector employment over the next few years as the Chancellor follows up ... with an emergency budget in June and a full spending review in the autumn.'

An earlier recession, points out the *FT*, in the early 1990s, when the deficit amounted to only £50 billion instead of the current £156 billion, saw cuts entailing 600,000 jobs 'as public sector employment fell from just under 5.4 million in 1991 to 4.8 million in 1998 before growing again'.

Baby bonds are being squeezed out to save £320 million in 2010, and £500 million the following year, when they are finally eliminated. Something around £290 million will be saved by ending payments to the Future Jobs Fund, which had aimed to create 110,000 jobs for unemployed youths. Thirty million pounds will be saved by cutting out a thousand pound subsidy to employers who take on the unemployed. A bonfire of smaller quangos will also be carried through.

But Lord Freud, the turncoat Minister for Welfare Reform, has confirmed that very much larger economies are in prospect, as he gets to grips with welfare budgets, eliminating £5.2 billion which are estimated to be expended on fraud and error, that is to say 'what we know about'. The implication is that there is more treasure still buried at the end of this rainbow. Is this all rhetoric aimed at assuaging the anxieties of the markets, or does it reflect a real commitment? Whatever it is, it does not represent 'the limit of our ambition' said Lord Freud. The Government plans to shift more than 2.5 million claimants off Incapacity Benefit to the new Employment and Support Allowance, which is to be accompanied by a huge welfare-to-work programme aimed at prising them into the labour market.

Small wonder that the Institute for Fiscal Studies pronounced its verdict that Britain now confronts 'the longest and deepest sustained period of cuts to public service spending since the Second World War'.

It fell to David Laws to present his appetiser for the cuts to come, in his first speech to the new Parliament. According to the British newspapers, the then Treasury Chief Secretary apologised for 'sorting out the mess in public finances'. Mr. Laws must have been surprised by the press he got, which presented him as a modern Demosthenes, railing against the over-mighty state, as if it were the evil Macedonian empire. Vigorous though our new axe man showed himself to be when faced with evil paupers, he shrank from more potent adversaries, such as the grossly excessive military budget.

Sacred cows, of course, remain sacred. Worse, the sacred Trident programme, in spite of Liberal Democrat protestations of virtue, and genteel threats to postpone if not asphyxiate it, remains firmly in place as the keystone of defence policy. During the Election, Generals queued up to question the sense of this policy. Immense treasure will be lavished on new aircraft carriers, as well as the necessary new submarines to carry the expensive new missiles with their regenerated warheads. None of these things will come cheap. Four of these important military commanders set their thoughts down for *The Times*:

> 'It is of deep concern that the question of the Trident replacement programme is at present excluded from this process [*of the Comprehensive Strategic Defence Review*]. With an estimated lifetime cost of more than £80 billion, replacing Trident will be one of the most expensive weapons programmes this country has seen. Going ahead will clearly have long-term consequence for the military and the defence equipment budget that need to be carefully examined.
>
> Given the present economic climate, in which the defence budget faces the prospect of worrying cuts, and that we have already an estimated hole in the defence equipment budget of some £35 billion, it is crucial that a review is fully costed and looks critically at all significant planned defence spending.
>
> The debate has shifted significantly since the 2007 decision to proceed with replacing Trident. Internationally there is a growing consensus that rapid cuts in nuclear forces, starting with the US and Russia, but with the smaller nuclear states following, is the way to achieve international security.
>
> There have been promising developments in the multilateral disarmament process led by President Obama, including the recent US-Russia nuclear arms reduction agreement.
>
> Through the Nuclear Threat Initiative and Global Zero, a powerful line-up of international statesmen, including Mikhail Gorbachev, Henry Kissinger and Desmond Tutu, have added their voices to the call for a nuclear-free world.
>
> Such a world would undoubtedly be a safer place, and while it remains a distant and challenging goal, opportunities to bring it closer should be given thorough consideration by any government.
>
> Serious concerns have also been raised by members of the services and defence analysts about the strategic value of nuclear weapons and their relevance to modern warfare. Indeed, three of us wrote to *The Times* on this subject in January 2009. These fundamental questions about how and against whom our nuclear weapons act as a deterrent must still he answered.
>
> The potential impact of a UK commitment to replace Trident on the international disarmament negotiations must also be considered along with its impression on other states. As the former head of the International Atomic Energy Authority Mohamed El Baradei put it: "It is very hard to preach the virtues of non-smoking when you have a cigarette dangling from your lips and you are about to buy a new pack."
>
> Any genuinely comprehensive review needs to weigh up all of these issues and answer the question: "Is the UK's security best served by going ahead with business as usual; reducing our nuclear arsenal; adjusting our nuclear posture or eliminating our nuclear weapons?"
>
> Should the review determine that there is still a need for a nuclear deterrent, a number of options may be more affordable than a like-for-like replacement of the Trident system, which has been described as a "Rolls-Royce" solution. The

state of the public finances requires each of these options to be carefully evaluated, alongside like-for-like replacement and disarmament.

It is no longer good enough to skirt round the question of what actual military value an expensive nuclear deterrent provides to our services by labelling the decision a "political one". This decision will have a direct impact on our overstretched Armed Forces. Allowing the military's views to be excluded from this decision will have consequences both predictable and regrettable.

It may well be that money spent on new nuclear weapons will be money that is not available to support our frontline troops, or for crucial counterterrorism work; money not available for buying helicopters, armoured vehicles, frigates or even for paying for more manpower.

Suppressing discussion of these issues or dismissing alternatives before properly examining them would be a big strategic blunder. All political parties must allow a full and open debate about the Trident replacement as part of the Strategic Defence Review.'

This broadside was signed by Field Marshall Lord Bramall, General Lord Ramsbotham, General Sir Hugh Beach and Major-General Patrick Cordingley.

The Generals are probably right that the budgetary constraints that are involved here may continue to ensure that foot soldiers may not receive the necessary boots in which to do their work. But some of us would like to keep the soldiers away from foreign deserts, and economise on boots as well as bombs. This means that the quarrels which divide the Labour Party remain by no means academic. The war in Iraq, and the senseless slaughter in Afghanistan, have not only outreached the liberal conscience, but also will bankrupt the neo-liberal treasury. How long before this happens? How soon can we expect to recover the wisdom of the late Harold Wilson, and withdraw from commitments East of Suez?

Paupers cannot afford to police the world, especially if that task requires that the world be subjugated again before imperial rule can hold sway. 'Not again!' is a good rule.

* * *

Somewhat heavily promoted in the Labour Party's leadership stakes is former Foreign Secretary David Miliband. In fact, some candidates had alleged that he was keeping quiet about the large number of nominations he had received, in order to minimise speculation that he has been the approved Blairite successor. Be that as it may, he has declared that the decision to invade Iraq in 2003 should not preoccupy the Labour Party in the discussions about its leadership. Two other candidates had criticised the decision to invade, and David Miliband said that it was 'time to move on' in response to their arguments. But many of us believe that the only onward move that might be morally acceptable would be to the trial of the perpetrators, who lied us into a massacre.

The argument will not be closed so easily. Miliband senior reiterates the old story that every intelligence service in the world insisted that Iraq had weapons of mass destruction. He has also insisted that he had, at the time, read the 174-page report of Hans Blix (the so-called 'Clusters Report'). His predecessor, Jack Straw, gave a tendentious account of this document which Hans Blix corrected:

> 'That report was an analysis of what Unscom (United Nations Special Commission) before us had found, and what we in our analysis had found. It put the cases of unresolved issues in clusters, and lined out what Iraqis could do to help us to solve them. There was nothing sensationally new in this document.'

The document says in its introduction:

> 'The principal part of this document thus presents clusters of "unresolved disarmament issues", which are to be addressed by the inspection process (and Iraq) and from which "key remaining disarmament tasks" are to be identified and selected for early solution.'

Chris Ames of *Iraq Inquiry Digest* recalled this fact when responding to the former Foreign Secretary:

> 'Which bit of "to be addressed by the inspection process" and "selected for early solution" did the allegedly very clever Miliband interpret as meaning: "cut short the inspections and invade Iraq"? And which bit of Blix's rebuttal of Straw did Miliband not get?'

Worse, the hoary old claim that the world's intelligence services were unanimous in asserting Iraq's ownership of weapons of mass destruction had been decisively refuted by Vladimir Putin in October 2002:

> 'Russia does not have in its possession any trustworthy data that supports the existence of nuclear weapons or any weapons of mass destruction in Iraq and we have not received any such information from our partners as yet.'

Neither, of course, had anyone else.

David Miliband cannot acknowledge the truth in these statements without repudiating Blair, which would mean repudiating the former leader's diminishing band of supporters, who may be rather important electors in this electorate.

There are signs that war hysteria is receding. Fewer and fewer are those prepared to admit that they were ever in favour of conquering Iraq, even if this would enable them to hang Saddam Hussein. More sturdy Liberals are discovering their long-term opposition to capital punishment, even for the demons of yesterday. The new upsurge of pacifism is also cautiously invading the Labour Party, where some leadership contenders seem to agree that there may not be many votes in future wars. Of course, the old wars were monstrosities, and should never have been begun. Several hundred thousand people have been killed, millions have been displaced, economies have been wrecked, and civil progress has been forced into panic-stricken retreat. There may at times have been some excesses in pacifist thought, but militarism has clearly been revealed as a murderous disorder in men's thinking.

The Labour Party will never recover until this begins to obtain due recognition, and its war drums are finally silenced.

But there is another re-evaluation which is vitally necessary to the recovery of political life in Britain. Socialism has to become again a normal part of political discourse. The decision to repudiate the Labour Party's Clause IV was presented as a revolt against archaic language. But archaic language could have been modernised without occasioning distress. No one was discussing the archaic language involved in the Ten Commandments, which could with profit have commended itself to Mr. Blair.

Cynics among us believe that the radical impulse to doing away with the Labour Party's constitutional commitment to some form of socialism was driven by the fashion for privatisation, and perhaps the desire that well-placed personages in the political firmament might also 'become filthy rich'. Be that as it may, now that *The Orange Book* rules, and an Orange Demosthenes can rant us all into more and more acute social distress, it is surely time that we must rediscover the antidote to market collapse, ruin in the banks, and capitalism in distress. The annulment of Clause IV notwithstanding, Labour nationalised failing banks. What terrifies surviving bankers is the thought that perhaps future governments might not be willing to follow this example. But who will agree to the reinvention of socialism as a last ditch saviour of an economic system in collapse? Might it not more commendably save the people?

That is why we devote some attention to the long lost issue of Clause IV, which served in earlier years to differentiate the emerging Labour Party from Liberal hegemony. The Liberals were the party of business, and the workers still tended to regard themselves as part of business, so that it was possible to invent Lib-Lab Members of Parliament. But the interests of business were not identical with those of employees, or the mass of the ordinary people. Today *The Orange Book* apostles are preaching a doctrine which makes this abundantly clear, and for those who are slow to learn, they are implementing policies to match. If there was never any socialism before, it would be necessary today to invent some.

Socialism has, for all that, left us all with a serious problem over the years: how do we socialise the entrepreneurial function? This problem is brought no nearer to solution by selling off the Post Office to the highest bidder, especially when that bidder may in fact have tendered an offer which is lower than low.

* * *

During this tumultuous meltdown of established verities, the newly discovered opposition has been trying to reorient itself. A number of left-wing Members of Parliament increased their votes during a General Election which saw the eclipse of several former stars of New Labour. It is true that two cheers have been heard, but the overall picture has not been encouraging. Alternative policies have been scarcely visible, and certainly insufficiently potent to challenge the new orthodoxy of neo-liberalism. True, Labour's neo-liberals have suffered a serious blow with the defection of *The Orange Book* reactionaries to the coalition. Their 'approach' is now discredited and in disarray. But the reincarnation of the Labour Party is by no means assured. It will be incredibly difficult to set in motion the reforms that could allow it to recuperate its strength from below. Swingeing changes have gravely undermined its former democracy. The Labour Party Conference has been not only housetrained, but broken, as all its effective powers have been leeched away.

The National Executive Committee, which was at times a strong upholder of the rights of the membership, has been taken over for the most part by poodles. Time was when new policies could be originated, quite literally, from the bottom up. Proposals put forward by ward parties could advance through the Constituencies up to the National Conference, and be carried into effect. A whole series of reforms of the Party structure were in fact initiated in precisely this way. No longer is this imaginable, unless the most serious changes can be initiated. And where could this be done but at the top of the Party? Its grassroots are parched and would find it difficult to identify green if ever they saw it. In this sense, what the Party would need to enter into a true recovery would be a process akin to *perestroika*.

It is true that reforms initiated from above can be blocked or reversed from above, unless they catch on and inspire new momentum among the democrats. Democracy requires not only self-confident advocacy, but a minimum sense of possibility, of openness to change. That is what is likely to be initiated from the top, or nowhere.

The famous perestroika began when the most powerful people in the Soviet Union, the heads of the security services with their political nominees, understood that things simply could not continue in the manner to which all had become accustomed. Can things in today's Labour Party continue as they were? All the talk about a political class originates from registering the changes in the Labour Party which have not only disenfranchised, but to a large extent excluded, the victims of political policy. What Mrs. Thatcher began, Mr. Blair effectively consolidated. Not for nothing did Mrs. Thatcher boast that New Labour was perhaps her greatest achievement.

It is an extreme example to look at the evolution of the coalfields, with the obliteration of independent-minded political action, the affliction of mass unemployment, and the consequent loss of hope. But I think of a formerly vital trade union branch secretary, who, in order to survive, had to accept a job on minimum possible wages as a Securicor official, and work every hour that was obtainable, Christmas Days and other holidays included. What scope had he to practise the skills he had earlier learnt in forming social policy and mobilising to develop it? I think of other miners, their talents unwanted and unrecognised, languishing on the sofas in their kitchens, whilst their children trooped out of the houses to school and back, also profoundly uncertain of their futures, and steeped in that deep pessimism that is secreted in this culture of neglect.

Yes, there have been new kinds of work, new skills, and new sources of optimistic development. But, entrapped in the prevailing areas of distress, such developments have not, as many anticipated, created a vibrant new culture of democratic self-expression, of human growth and development, of confidence in our collective powers. In a way, New Labour was the political expression of this demoralisation, and the annulment of confident democracy in the Labour Party is its result. As it blanketed the country its influence was uneven: pockets of self-assertion remained. Freedom could never be completely extinguished. But institutionally, modern Labour is now virtually devoid of social aspirations. It is going nowhere: it offers freedom to none but the political classes themselves, and that freedom is a poor, stunted, miserably acquisitive and unhappy experience.

There remain large numbers of Socialists seeking forms of association that might give them the influence that they would need to associate those who wish to pioneer new social forms. But they, too, are mired in deep difficulties, because, not unnaturally, they seek comprehensive solutions to the problems which have beset the overall Labour movement. The search for the one true way never stops. But if it is allowed to pose each reformer against all, then the one true way will never be found, because that way lies in democratic association itself, and only an ample movement which encourages both thought and action will ever permit it to be found.

We cannot create the perfect revolution in the village hall, but it might be in the village hall that we can agree on a common approach to sorting out a wide variety of problems, and maybe not only local ones, in collaboration. Raising our sights may then become possible.

It could be that no one will recuperate the Labour Party, in which case it will continue to shrink into ever-diminishing circles of recrimination and despair. But if it were possible to light again the flame of democratic aspiration, then no one can be sure that its finest days are not yet to come.

Ken Coates

ASLEF the train drivers' union

www.aslef.org.uk

The Tories are pro-Trident

The Lib Dems are anti-Trident

Their 'joint' government is pro-Trident

That's the Coalition – and the 'new politics' – in a nutshell!

They're all Tories ... !

Keith Norman
General Secretary

Alan Donnelly
President

Clause IV

Sidney Webb

This is the first of three articles picking up on the editorial discussion of common ownership and the Labour Party. It was originally written for The Observer, *to explain the thinking behind Sidney Webb's proposals for a new constitution for the Labour Party. It was published in 1917. The constitution was adopted the following year.*

◄ *Ken Coates with Labour Leader John Smith.*

The proposal to reorganise the Labour Party, formulated by its National Executive, and circulated to its constituent societies for their consideration, may well prove an event of far-reaching political importance. Instead of a sectional and somewhat narrow group, what is aimed at is now a national party, open to anyone of the 16,000,000 electors agreeing with the party programme.

More important, however, than any of these changes in the constitution is the change of spirit that has inspired them. The Labour Party, which has never been formally restricted to manual-working wage-earners, is now to be publicly thrown open to all workers 'by hand or by brain'.

Its declared object is to be, not merely the improvement of the conditions of the wage-earner, but 'to secure for the producers, by hand or by brain, the full fruits of their industry and the most equitable distribution thereof that may be possible upon the basis of the common ownership of the means of production, and the best obtainable system of popular administration and control of each industry or service'.*

The only persons to be excluded (and that, of course, only by inference) are the unoccupied and unproductive recipients of rents and dividends – the so-called 'idle rich' – whom it is interesting to find *The Times* editorially declaring to be of no use to the community.

The Labour Party of the future, in short, is to be a party of the producers, whether

---

* 'Historical Note: The 'distribution and exchange' were added to Clause IV of the Labour Party constitution in 1929. They were moved as amendments to the Constitution by the Bristol Labour Party and went through without any debate.

manual workers or brain workers, associated against the private owners of land and capital as such. Its policy of 'common ownership' brings it, as a similar evolution brought John Stuart Mill – to use his own words in the *Autobiography* – 'decidedly under the general designation of Socialist'. But it is a Socialism which is no more specific than a definite repudiation of the individualism that characterised all the political parties of the past generation and that still dominates the House of Commons.

This declaration of the Labour Party leaves it open to choose from time to time whatever forms of common ownership from the co-operative store to the nationalised railway, and whatever forms of popular administration and control of industry, from national guilds to ministries of employment and municipal management, may, in particular cases, commend themselves.

What the Labour Party at present means by its Socialism is revealed in the remarkable pamphlet which it has published on its 'After the War Programme', setting forth in a dozen detailed resolutions passed at the Manchester Party Conference exactly what it wishes done with the railways, the canals, the coal mines, the banking system, the demobilisation of the army and munition workers, the necessary rehousing of the people, the measures to be taken for preventing the occurrence of unemployment, the improvement of agriculture, the taxation to be imposed to pay for the war, the reform of our educational system, and what not.

Opinions will naturally differ as to some of these sweeping proposals, but no one of any education can safely denounce them as unpractical or despise them as ill-informed.

It is, indeed, one of the claims of the Labour Party that science is on their side; that it is their proposals, not those of the Liberals or those of the Unionists, that nowadays receive the general support of the 'orthodox' economists; and that, as a matter of fact, it is essentially their proposals to which every Minister of State, when he is brought up against a difficult problem of administration, has actually to turn – and then to lose his nerve, emasculate what would have got over his difficulties, and produce an abortion which has the advantages neither of individualism nor of collectivism!

But the programme of the Labour Party is, and will probably remain, less important (except for educating the political leaders of other parties) than the spirit underlying the programme, that spirit which gives any party its soul.

The Labour Party stands essentially for revolt against the inequality of circumstance that degrades and brutalises and disgraces our civilisation. It abhors and repudiates the unscientific and immoral doctrine that the competitive struggle for the means of life is, in human society, either inevitable or requisite for the survival of the fittest; it declares, indeed, in full accord with science, that competition produces degradation and death, whilst it is conscious and deliberate co-operation which is productive of life and progress.

It is unreservedly democratic in its conviction – here also fortified by political science – that only by the widest possible participation in power and the most generally spread consciousness of consent can any civilised community attain either its fullest life or its utmost efficiency. But it recognises that no mere rightness of aspiration or morality or purpose can in themselves accomplish their ends; and that for the achievement of results, knowledge and the application of the scientific method is required, notably in the science of society, for the further study and endowment of which it presses.

And finally the Labour Party has faith in internationalism (as distinguished from the characteristically liberal cosmopolitanism). It repudiates all 'Imperialism' or desire for domination over other races. It pleads for the right of each people to live its own life, and make its own specific contribution to the world in its own way, recognising, indeed, no one 'superior race' but 'reciprocal superiorities' among all races.

It is not without significance that the National Executive of the Labour Party has included, as a fundamental object of the Party, the establishment of a Federation or League of Nations for such international legislation as may prove possible. No other political party has yet nailed this flag to its mast.

The Labour Party is, without doubt, today the party of inspiration and promise. Tomorrow it may well prove to be the party of the future, destined, perhaps, to play as large a part in the political history of the twentieth century as the Liberal Party did in that of the nineteenth.

*   *   *

There follows the complete text of Clause IV of the Constitution of the Labour Party. Item 7 was added at the suggestion of Tony Benn, during the time of the Gaitskell leadership of the late 1950s. The text follows Webb's 1917-18 draft, as changed in 1929.

1. Clause IV

The objects of the Labour Party are set out in Clause IV of the party's constitution. It reads as follows:

National
1. To organise and maintain in parliament and in the country a political Labour Party.
2. To co-operate with the General Council of the Trades Union Congress,

or other kindred organisations, in joint political or other action in harmony with the party constitution and standing orders.
3. To give effect as far as maybe practicable to the principles from time to time approved by the party conference.
4. To secure for the workers by hand or by brain the full fruits of their industry and the most equitable distribution thereof that may be possible upon the basis of the common ownership of the means of production, distribution, and exchange, and the best obtainable system of popular administration and control of each industry or service.
5. Generally to promote the political, social and economic emancipation of the people, and more particularly of those who depend directly upon their own exertions by hand or by brain for the means of life.

Inter-Commonwealth
6. To co-operate with the labour and socialist organisations in the Commonwealth overseas with a view to promoting the purposes of the party, and to take common action for the promotion of a higher standard of social and economic life for the working population of the respective countries.

International
7. To co-operate with the labour and socialist organisations in other countries and to support the United Nations Organisation and its various agencies and other international organisations for the promotion of peace, the adjustment and settlement of international disputes by conciliation or judicial arbitration, the establishment and defence of human rights, and the improvement of the social and economic standards and conditions of work of the people of the world.

* * *

These three articles were published in Clause IV: Common Ownership and the Labour Party *by Ken Coates MEP (Spokesman Books, 1995, £6.99).*

'We cannot administer capitalism because we don't believe in it!'

Clement Attlee

This second article was written some 20 years after Webb's. When there was a serious prospect of an electoral alliance between Labour and the Liberals, during the 1930s, it took the form of calls for a 'popular front' against the Conservatives. Clement Attlee had recently been elected leader of the Labour Party. This is how he evaluated the project in the Left Book Club's The Labour Party in Perspective.

The Labour Party stands for such great changes in the economic and social structure that it cannot function successfully unless it obtains a majority which is prepared to put its principles into practice. Those principles are so far-reaching that they affect every department of the public services and every phase of policy. The plain fact is that a Socialist Party cannot hope to make a success of administering the Capitalist system because it does not believe in it. This is the fundamental objection to all the proposals that are put forward for the formation of a Popular Front in this country.

There are many people who suggest that what is required at the present time is the formation of an alliance between all the Left Wing forces in order to get rid of the present Government. The argument is based sometimes on the need for getting through certain urgent reforms in home affairs, sometimes, and perhaps more frequently, on the plea that at all events all can unite on a common policy in foreign affairs, and that on this basis it would be possible to rally a majority in this country for what is vaguely called a Left Government. Many people stress the purely negative attitude – that is to say, the urgent need of getting rid of the present administration before, through their feeble and dishonest policy, they allow the world to be plunged into war. Others believe that it is possible to form a short-term policy to which the various Left Wing groups would give their adhesion, and that upon this basis electoral arrangements could be made which would ensure a majority.

I would not myself rule out such a thing

as an impossibility in the event of the imminence of a world crisis. It might on a particular occasion be the lesser of two evils, but it is worth while examining these proposals in some detail, because they have an appeal to many who do not in my view look far enough ahead.

I will first deal with the purely negative proposal which considers that the really vital thing is the extrusion from power of the present Government. I should be the last person to underrate the importance of this, but the overthrow of the present Government means its replacement by another. You cannot simply leave a vacuum.

A majority of heterogeneous composition returned on a negative policy of turning the Government out, with a clear foreign policy but no programme for home affairs, would not last more than a few weeks. Even where foreign affairs overshadow the political scene, the day to day work of a Government is mainly concerned with administration and legislation on internal affairs. The essential support that a Government needs is not for a few major issues, but for the ordinary common round and daily task. The first essential for a Government which has to work through the House of Commons is command over time. More things are lost by delay than by open opposition. The elaborate machinery of the Whips Office, and the discipline imposed on the supporters of a Government, are essential if it is to function at all. This discipline, although enforced by pains and penalties, by hopes of reward and by the fear of dissolution, depends in the last resort far more on a realisation by the members of the relative importance of particular issues. The discipline imposed by membership of a party not only in the House of Commons, but in constituency party work, is a reflection of a general appraisement of the value of the attainment of certain aims, and a willingness to subordinate the particular points on which the individual feels keenly to the general sense of the Party. It is, in fact, the acceptance of the fundamental principle of democracy – majority rule.

It has never been easy to obtain this discipline in parties of the Left. Parties of the Right tend to contain fewer individualities, while their members in this country have been drilled by the nature of their upbringing to the acceptance of what they would term the team spirit. Parties of the Left tend to be composed of enthusiasts for particular reforms who hope by joining with others to achieve their aims, and of men and women who have through their individuality come to the front, rather than those who by the possession of wealth or position have drifted into politics. Thus the Liberal Party always tended to be fissiparous. It always included in its ranks a number of what are called impolitely 'cranks' – that is to say, enthusiasts for various good causes. The party was kept together by the large body of persons who were traditional Liberals, or perhaps even without any market convictions except an interest in politics and a desire to make a career.

In the Labour Party, the Trade Union element serves as the solid core of disciplined membership. The loyalty to majority decisions, which is the foundation of industrial action, takes the place of what is called among Conservatives the team spirit, while long training in the responsibilities of Trade Union work has induced a habit of mind which realises the practical necessity for compromise in non-essentials. A further link which makes for united action is the common faith in Socialism which inspires the members. There are, however, always a few who, while convinced Socialists, have as their main incentive devotion to some particular reform. Their enthusiasm for their own special cause is apt at times to make them lose their sense of proportion. There are also, naturally, some members whose fervent desire for the achievement of their ideals makes them impatient of the delays and partial successes which are inevitable in working through the methods of parliamentary democracy.

The experience of the two Labour Governments showed how difficult it was for many of these to accept the compromises inseparable from all Government, but particularly from a Government in a minority. There was needed to give the experiment the degree of success which it attained the full force of party loyalty and of devotion to the cause of Socialism.

But if there is to be an election resulting in the return of a majority consisting of several minorities united only on a negative, the Government will be intolerably weak. If the groups are in themselves strong and coherent, it may be possible, by the inclusion of leaders drawn from all of them, to obtain a fairly consistent support, but at best the battle will only be transferred from the floor of the House and party meetings to the Cabinet Room. The larger the party the greater its sense of responsibility; the smaller the group the more irresponsible. The largest party becomes at once the prisoner of the minority groups, which put all the pressure they can to ensure decisions in the sense which they desire ...

Many of these objections apply equally to the suggestion that there should be a positive programme to which all organisations on the Left should adhere. It is thought that many Liberals might accept a limited programme of certain specific items calculated to be carried through within the life of one Parliament, and that upon this basis a Left Government might be achieved at an early date. It is thought that there is a large body of Left opinion which, while unwilling to commit itself to Socialism, is yet prepared to accept a considerable instalment of the

Socialist programme. It is commonly suggested that enough work for one Parliament could be found without going beyond the limits which would repel adherents of the Capitalist system.

It must be admitted that there is considerable strength of opinion in support of this proposition, and I think that there is ground for the view that there are many in this country who are prepared to go a long way with the Labour Party while not prepared to take the plunge and join any affiliated organisation. It is, therefore, worth while examining this proposition.

The first question that arises is as to the limits of the programme which would be acceptable. I find that the proposition often reduces itself to this – that if the Labour Party would drop its Socialism and adopt a Liberal platform, many Liberals would be pleased to support it. I have heard it said more than once that if Labour would only drop its policy of nationalisation everyone would be pleased, and it would soon obtain a majority.

I am convinced that it would be fatal for the Labour Party to form a Popular Front on any such terms. It may be possible in other countries, but not in this. I have stated above that Socialists cannot make Capitalism work. The 1929 experiment demonstrated this. No really effective steps could be taken to deal with the economic crisis, because any attempt to deal with fundamentals brought opposition from the Liberals. Labour men who saw clearly the need for dealing with causes had to try to deal with results. The amount that could be extracted for the workers from a Capitalist system was limited. When this limit had been reached, failure was bound to ensue. I admit that the experiment was not made under fair conditions. The Party was handicapped by the conditions of the time, which demanded drastic measures, and by its leading personnel, who had surrendered their minds to Capitalism long before they sold their bodies.

Therefore any such short programme to be acceptable to Socialists must contain measures which will take the country a long way on the road to the desired goal. It must contain a big instalment of nationalisation. The subjects of nationalisation must be not those about which there is little controversy, because they are not vital, but those which are really vital for the transformation of society and are called for in the national interest. I shall indicate later what I believe these to be, but I do not know how far it would be possible for any large number of Liberals to accept them.

Next, there must be a development of the control of the community over trade and industry, which runs counter to the shibboleths of individualism. I do not underrate the value of the suspicion of bureaucracy which the Liberals exhibit. It is, indeed, necessary that Socialists should import into the structure of the society which they are building what is valid in Liberalism, but I have the impression that Liberal elements in a Popular Front Government would baulk at necessary controls.

With this there must be a steady pressure exerted through the medium of the Budget, wage standards, social services, etc., towards a more equalitarian society. I return to the point which I made above – that in the carrying on of a Government it is all-round support that is required. A Socialist Government must inform its whole administration with the socialist ideal. All its Ministers must be conscious of the goal to which they are steering the ship of State. It is just here that I see the crux of the situation. In a Popular Front the Socialist elements are definitely out to replace Capitalism by Socialism. They work with that aim in view all the time. If, on the other hand, they have colleagues or supporters whose conscious aim is the preservation of Capitalism, there cannot possibly be harmony.

There are those who will say that this is a playing with words; that 'We are all Socialists now'; that there is no absolute Socialism or Capitalism; that it is all a matter of degree and so forth. I cannot accept this. Socialism to me is not just a piece of machinery or an economic system, but a living faith translated into action. I desire the classless society, and the substitution of the motive of service for that of competition. I must, therefore, differ in my outlook from the man who still clings to the present system. Even though we agree that, say, the mines should be nationalised, we disagree with the end in view and with the reason for our action. He regards the mining industry as an exception to the general way he wishes to carry on industry. He thinks that owing to the history and conditions of the industry it had better be nationalised, but he still regards it as a profit-making undertaking. I, on the other hand, conceive it as a basic activity of the community or providing certain necessary needs, and as but the first of many services which must undergo a transformation.

Blair's Initiative
Revising socialism or rejecting it?

Ken Coates

Sixty years on, in 1995, Tony Blair's promise to the Labour Party of a discussion on new objectives was not to be honoured in the way members originally expected. A very one-sided presentation was circulated throughout the Party.

Introducing their new statement on 'Labour's Objects: Socialist Values in the Modern World', the Blair leadership team offer us a preliminary statement which tells us that 'the Labour Party is a democratic socialist party'. This goes on to offer a menu which could be presented by almost any Liberal:

> 'It is founded on the simple belief that individuals prosper when supported by a strong and active society, and that people owe a duty to each other as well as themselves. It is from this central belief that our core values are derived: social justice, freedom, opportunity, equality, democracy and solidarity. Democratic socialism sees economic efficiency and social justice as complementary to one another, not opposites; and links together action to establish a prosperous and strong economy with action to attack poverty, increase employment, counter discrimination, curb unaccountable power, and protect the environment.'

What is wrong with such a liberal prospectus? Certainly most of the objects appeal to elementary commonsense. Why is that insufficient?

If democratic socialism 'sees economic efficiency and social justice as complementary to one another, not opposites', what measures does it propose to ensure that its vision begins to correspond to reality? Left alone, economic efficiency as it is conventionally understood stands in no relation whatever to social justice because it is not driven by either law or compassion, but by competition for growth and survival. Aneurin Bevan once summed it up with admirable economy:

> 'What are the most worthy objects on which to spend surplus productive capacity? ...

After providing for the kind of life we have been leading as a social aggregate, there is an increment left over that we can use as we wish. What would we like to do with it?

Now the first thing to notice is that in a competitive society this question is never asked. It is not a Public question at all. It cannot be publicly asked with any advantage because it is not capable of a public decision which can be carried out. Therefore in this most vital sphere, the shaping of the kind of future we would like to lead, we are disfranchised at the very outset. We are unable to discuss it because the disposal of the economic surplus is not ours to command ... The surplus is merely a figure of speech. Its reality consists of a million and one surpluses in the possession of as many individuals ... If we reduce the question to the realm where we have brought it, that is to say, to the individual possessor of the surplus, the economist will provide us with a ready answer. He will tell us that the surplus owner will invest it in the goods for which he thinks there will be a profitable sale. The choice will lie with those able to buy the goods the owner of the surplus will proceed to produce. This means that those who have been most successful for the time being, the money owners, will in the sum of their individual decisions determine the character of the economy of the future ... But ... the kind of society which emerges from the sum of individual choices is not one which commends itself to the generality of men and women. It must be borne in mind that the successful were not choosing a type of society. They were only deciding what they thought could be bought and sold profitably.' (*In Place of Fear*)

That is to say, social priorities, including social justice, cannot be assured simply by reliance on the market. This possesses no self-corrective mechanism for transferring individual surpluses 'to attack poverty, increase employment, counter discrimination, curb unaccountable power, and protect the environment'.

'Justice' has to be *outside* the market, and presupposes a capacity by the public authority to override it. But the market has been systematically eroding and dissolving all external pressures to regulate or control its operations for many years. In this respect it has enjoyed very considerable success.

In the past, action for correction could be taken, not by the market, but by Government. In pursuit of these social goals, Government might, by taxing profits and high incomes, transfer the revenue so garnered to good redistributive effect. But the Labour Party's present front bench insists that it proposes no structural shift in taxation other than the blocking of 'loopholes' ...

The new leadership statement has achieved on paper something that generations of supporters of Clause IV have never dreamt of. It has abolished capitalism. Nowhere can this dread concept be found in the new text. 'The process of constitutional revision', say the authors, 'is intended to set out our identity as a Party in our own terms for our own age'. But has capitalism really disappeared in this age of comforting and empty froth? It is true that capital has become more fluid, more mobile. At the touch of a button, millions can travel along the wires, or along the optical fibres, to disappear here and materialise in another place. Along the wires, routine tasks are transferred to low-paid Indian women, who programme the bookings for European airlines, and flash the resultant effort back in seconds. Then the prosperous stockholders can board their planes. Reality has not disappeared, but it has been beautifully concealed. Has Tony Blair got access to some of these computer buttons? Will the wires transmit his commands? And will they deliver social justice on all the screens that matter?

Alas, no. The present Labour leadership resembles nothing more than the inhabitants of those South Sea Islands which initiated the cargo cults. Observing that the missionaries who came among them lived very happy lives, the indigenous peoples made a close study of the causes of this happiness. They perceived that the missionaries wanted for nothing, and that the secret of their prosperity lay in the cargos which were ferried to them in small aeroplanes, at regular intervals. In the cargo, there was nourishment and uplift. Commentaries on scripture and crates of gin brought consolation to the foreign teachers.

Having scientific minds, the natives were quick to agree that the benefits of cargoes might with profit be more widely shared among the excluded. They gathered their forces, and cleared space in the forests, where the planes could land. They lit beacons, to guide them in. And they waited. But no cargoes came.

The long suffering people of Britain do not have so long to wait. No cargoes are coming. Unless remedial action is taken to redistribute wealth, the poor will decline into even deeper misery. And unless a strong public force generates local enterprise, stimulates co-operation, and encourages common effort, capitalism will assiduously ensure the continuation of present trends. More polarisation, richer rich, poorer poor. These processes will continue with a Queen or without one, with hereditary Peers, or without them, and throughout whatever cosmetic changes might be made to keep hidden the realities of economic power. Is that the modern age, or isn't it?

* * *

The history presented in the draft document is, to say the least of it, eccentric. It correctly informs us that the first draft of Clause IV appeared in October 1917, the very month of the Bolshevik Revolution. But it goes on to tell us that central planning 'had after all helped Britain to win the war'. Not in October 1917 it hadn't. Neither in 1917 had the Russian Soviets established public ownership and central planning. Their first task, under a variety of forms of workers' control, was to re-establish any kind of production, with or without the help of experienced managers. In 1917 and early 1918, the current of thought that constituted a perceived threat to the Labour leadership was syndicalist, and it seemed threatening because it advocated workers' control in British factories and industries, not in those of Russia or elsewhere.

The preliminary draft for the Clause had been written by Arthur Henderson. It spoke about taking into public ownership 'the monopolies'. This was a long-standing commitment of Henderson's, and it was based, not on socialist doctrine, but on impeccable Victorian liberal teaching. In the philosophical writings of T.H. Green, it had been pointed out that the Hegelian justification of property as 'the first reality of freedom' could no longer be invoked if property was monopolised. This is an old argument, which goes back a long way in political theory. Certainly Marx had identified the same problem that Green treated decades later. Locke had insisted, by contrast, that property was justified where men had 'mixed their labour' with the gifts of nature. But this, too, hit a problem with monopoly. What could happen when all the land was occupied, and none was left vacant to be mixed with the labour of any newcomer? This was the great fascination of America, as a seemingly inexhaustible source of virgin land, in which work would generate property, and thus in Hegelian terms, freedom. But monopoly closed out newcomers, bolted the door against them. From guaranteeing freedom, such property had become inimical to it. Thus, Henderson's formula was a direct echo of more than one important strand of liberal thinking. But Webb's amended version of Clause IV cut that link.

Webb was drawing on the experience of trade unionism during the First World War, and the growth of collectivist responses.

For many workers, the years of the war marked their first experience of something approaching humane working conditions. Employers became more than willing to strike reasonable bargains with their workpeople, because many of them were now remunerated on a 'cost-plus' system which guaranteed all munitions manufacturers a fixed rate of profit over and above the costs they incurred in production. Higher wages were simply higher costs, and offered no detriment to the 'plus' which would be allocated to profits.

Of course the founding fathers lived always in an ambivalent relationship to Liberalism. They were deeply engaged in the commitment to individual freedom, and to the need to create scope for all to become whatever each had it in himself or herself to be. But personal advance, for most, already depended on collective betterment.

Why did Webb's wording prevail? I was precisely attuned to the trade union experience of collective advance in this kind of planned war economy, and it was finely calculated to separate trade union voters from any residual allegiance they might feel to the Liberals as a Party. Since the working class electorate was considerably enlarged in 1918, this was a crucial strategic move.

If Clause IV served to demarcate Labour from the Liberal Party in 1918, what would its removal signify in 1995? Evidently it would mean realignment, in which Liberals of either the Liberal or Conservative Parties might feel free to participate.* How participate? By voting? By supporting? By joining in a common Party? By forming a common Government? And what might the programme of such a Government be? Who would represent the unemployed, the excluded, the poor, in such an enterprise? What mechanisms would exist to aid these groups of people? And who could represent the other employees? How many of them should be nudged downwards below the poverty barrier?

Capitalism may have become invisible behind its apparatus of wires and high-tech communication. It may no longer have its national roots. It has certainly disappeared from the programme of 'New Labour', which never comes near to mentioning it. But until it is displaced from its authority over our economic life, it will still call all the tunes.

The historical section of the leadership statement tells us that Clause IV was agreed because 'there was genuine revulsion at the sheer anarchy and exploitation associated with the free-market of Victorian capitalism'. And the anarchy of modern global capitalism? The destruction of large parts of the world economy, mass starvation and civil war in former colonies across Africa, and here at home seven and a half million *long-term* unemployed in the territories of the European Community alone: is there no anarchy and exploitation there? Large tracts of Britain are crumbling into physical and moral ruins. Do we need to do sums to explain this?

Nobody, but nobody, in the Labour movement, will seek to hamper any Labour leadership, if it will tell us how it will restore hope to the forgotten people of Britain, and join forces with others to help the destitute in Africa and elsewhere. A programme for this kind of action could conceivably be an 'adequate expression of what the Labour Party stands for'. But such an expression will not only mention the word capitalism. It will try to analyse what has happened to capital, and seek to find appropriate ways to curtail the immense concentrations of power which it has secreted.

---

* All this has been justified in the name of Antonio Gramsci as a recipe for the creation of what is unappealingly described as a 'hegemonic bloc'. Poor Gramsci is revolving in his grave. It is strange to see this most principled and democratic of all Western Communists pressed into service by the most unprincipled and manipulative of all opportunists.

Ken Coates

1930-2010

Tony Topham with Ken Coates and Ron Todd at the launch of their History of the Transport and General Workers' Union *in 1991.*

A Flower of the Labour Movement

Many spontaneous tributes to Ken Coates were published when his death was announced in June 2010. We reprint a small selection, together with excerpts from those made at Ken's funeral in Chesterfield, which was attended by more than 200 people.

I thought of, I think of Ken, as a venerable spreading tree under which we could sit, and, sitting there, learn what to do.

John Berger

He was a wonderful person, and will be sorely missed.

Noam Chomsky

* * *

Ken was one of the best and most influential socialist activists, politicians, and writers of the European Left. From the Institute for Workers' Control, the Bertrand Russell Peace Foundation, European Nuclear Disarmament, the European Appeal for Full Employment, to Socialist Renewal, he played a leading part in the Left and the labour movement.

Rare are people with such gifts: Ken combined a superb grasp of abstract economic and political issues, with the ability to organise within the broad trade union movement and peace campaigners. His experience as a coal miner (never worn as a trump against 'intellectuals'), his easy relations with ordinary working people, and his enduring commitment to grass-roots activity, earned him great respect.

I came into direct contact with Ken during his period as a Member of the European Parliament (1989 to 1999). The European Full Employment Conventions (both held in Brussels at the Parliament) had a wide echo. Attending them both was to realise just how widely and deeply Ken was respected. The delegation from Southern England (filling a coach from London) was made up of the kind of salt-of-the-earth left and union activists that keep our movement going. The Full Employment Appeal itself – which demanded decent levels of benefit and real job creation – is particularly relevant during the present economic crisis, and an answer to calls to slash-and-burn the public sector.

Ken stood four-square in the tradition of democratic socialism and promoted the self-management principles of workers' control with brio. He was evicted from the Labour Party (1998) over his protests with Hugh Kerr against dropping Clause Four. Efforts to form an alternative through the Independent Labour Network were not succesful. However, the steady stream of pamphlets from *Socialist Renewal*, his articles and books, and the journal/publishing house, *Spokesman*, continued. They interested, and will keep interesting, a wide public.

Like many on the left with similar views I have scores and scores of letters from Ken (the most recent was a written reply to an email about a year back). Ken seems never to have really trusted the Web for writing. His ability to engage in constant dialogue pre-dated Blogs, Newsgroups and Facebook. It was just one of the aspects that made him so deeply rooted in the best sides of the European, and world, socialist tradition.

Ken Coates was a *flower of the labour movement.*

He leaves behind comrades with warm memories and a determination to build on his achievements.

Andrew Coates
(tendancecoatesy.wordpress.com)

* * *

Inspiration

Andy Newman posted this tribute on the Socialist Unity website, under the title 'The Legacy of Ken Coates'.

I never knew Ken Coates personally, but I was sad to read of his recent passing. He played a very important role in the development of left ideas within the Labour Party.

During the 1960s, the traditional Bevanite left of the Party were increasingly staid, and identified state ownership as an end in itself. For example, Michael Foot in an interview with *New Left Review* in 1968 responded to the critics of the New Left by saying that there was nothing wrong with the strategy of corporate state ownership and Keynesianism economics, the problem was only the failure of Labour governments to implement the programme vigorously enough. Insofar as there was a mainstream radical alternative within the Labour Party it was from revisionists such as Crosland, Jay and Jenkins, who wanted to see less emphasis on the issues of state ownership, and more determination to pursue goals of fighting disadvantage and inequality.

Ken Coates was a vital figure, because he rejected the complacency and social conservatism of the Bevanites from the left, but determined to stay in the Labour Party, rather than go into what he saw as the self-righteous political wilderness of the New Left.

He was instrumental in 1968 in establishing the Institute for Workers Control, in conjunction with the publication *Voice of the Unions*, and various academics and activists. Prominent supporters of the IWC included Hugh Scanlon and Jack Jones, who were elected to become the leaders of the engineers and TGWU in 1967 and 1969.

Alongside his colleague, Tony Topham, Coates tirelessly argued in books and pamphlets for different models of social ownership, as opposed to the Morrisonian reality of state owned corporations in the same form as private corporations.

Coates argued that

> 'Workers' control brings back into the working class ... all that tremendous weight of self-esteem, of self recognition, of self respect, which has been stripped away by years of bureaucratic intrigues and manoeuvres in political institutions.'

Vitally, Ken Coates saw the need to develop practical alternative policies which could be pursued by working people, which were both pragmatic, but challenged the logic of the market. The Lucas Plan from the 1970s is the most famous example, for alternative production to meet social needs. As such, Ken Coates was a key intellectual and organising figure for the revival of the left in the Labour Party in the early 1980s.

He was elected as a Labour MEP in 1989, and did ten years of well respected work in the European Parliament. He was an outspoken critic of New Labour, which represented the attempt to negate his entire life's work and, scandalously, he was expelled from the Party in 1998, alongside Hugh Kerr MEP.

Ken Coates will be remembered as an inspiration, not just as a personal example, but because his ideas remain vital and relevant, and will continue to inform debate on the left for years to come.

* * *

It is with much emotion that I learned about Ken's death. I have always seen him as a man of exception, constantly involved in the promotion of peace and justice throughout the world.

Of course, it is in this spirit that we will continue the work of the Russell Tribunal on Palestine, for which he greatly helped us.

Pierre Galand, Russell Tribunal on Palestine

* * *

From Italy

For the Italian peace movement, Ken Coates was a friend who never let you down, and always taught you something new. It was Ken who first warned us that Cruise missiles were about to be deployed in the Comiso military base, at a time when most of us didn't even know where Comiso was. We found it on the map, in Sicily – in the very south of a continent which, at that time, in the early 1980s, was still divided in two military blocs bent upon the mad intent of pursuing MAD – Mutually Assured Destruction (that was the meaning of the acronym), and of so-called nuclear deterrence. An arms race which brought Cruise and Pershing missiles to the West (from Comiso to Greenham Common), and SS20s to Eastern Europe, triggering a new peace movement all over the Continent, from the Atlantic to the Urals. That movement changed the hearts and minds of millions of Europeans, stopped the arms race, and helped bring down the Berlin Wall. That movement had leaders such as Ken Coates of the Bertrand Russell Peace Foundation, and coordinator, with Luciana Castellina, of the European Nuclear Disarmament campaign. Ken was with us when we decided to hold the END Convention in Perugia, in 1984: not only among West Europeans, but also with the representatives of Eastern Europe, engaged in a difficult struggle for peace, freedom, and the end of dictatorship.

Later, in the ten years when Ken sat in the European Parliament, we knew we could always turn to him for advice and support, and for new initiatives against the new faces of War, be it in Iraq or the Balkans, in Sudan or the Middle East.

We will sorely miss him: but next year, when we celebrate the 50th anniversary of the first Peace March from Perugia to Assisi, we will certainly feel his presence, marching along with us as he had done so many times, with other friends we have lost, from E.P. Thompson to Lucio Lombardo Radice, from Alex Langer to Tom Benetollo, hand in hand with a new generation of activists ready to face the challenge of a new Europe in a new world, free from war, injustice and oppression.

Luciana Castellina, Chiara Ingrao, Flavio Lotti, Raffaella Bolini, Raffaella Chiodo, Luisa Morgantini, Giampiero Rasimelli and some 200 others

RESOLUTE
i.m. Ken Coates

One more good man gone!
Haiku he liked – hence, alas,
this briefest tribute.

Alexis Lykiard

* * *

From Greece

We express our deep sorrow for the sudden death of your Foundation's President, Ken Coates.

A great figure of the peace and anti-nuclear movement, of the British and European Left, was lost. A man who started as a miner, in 1948, and became an intellectual with many writings; a true internationalist and consistent supporter of the Greek people's struggle for democracy, peace and national independence.

Ken Coates was a close associate of the philosopher Bertrand Russell, whose work he continued at the frontlines of the peace movement in the difficult Cold War years. During the crucial 1980s decade, he played a decisive and leading role for the creation of END, the European Nuclear Disarmament movement.

Ken Coates believed in the European coordination of social movements, as well as of the European Left. In this framework our roads met and we worked together in many struggles, in the movements and in the European Parliament, where he was one of the most active members during 1989-99.

We will also remember him as a distinguished friend of our Party, who had come to Greece to support our political activities.

The loss of Ken Coates is great in the present crucial period that the European working people are faced with an unprecedented attack against their gains and rights. We will keep his ideas and fighting spirit as a very valuable source of inspiration in our efforts to promote the broadest possible fronts on a European level against neo-liberalism and euro-atlanticism.

Alexis Tsipras
President of SYNASPISMOS-Greece
(Coalition of the Left of Movements and Ecology)

A meeting in honour of Ken Coates will be held in Athens
on 21 September 2010, the International Day of Peace

* * *

From the Union

All of us here at Unite – particularly the former T&G section of it – were deeply saddened to hear of the death of Ken.

His contribution to our movement over so many years, and to the T&G, was immense. Ken was a man of great principle who never failed to take a stand for all that is of value in our movement. Many of us recall with admiration his work for peace and disarmament, and his efforts to keep the Labour Party true to its socialist roots. Had he been listened to more, many of the disasters associated with New Labour would surely have been avoided!

In the old T&G we owe a special debt to Ken as the co-author of the magnificent history of the union's formation and foundation. It set a standard for labour history that has never been surpassed and probably never will be, and revealed on every page his understanding of what makes a great working-class organisation tick. For that alone, future generations will thank him. All of us here would wish to be worthy of the great history he wrote, and the values he stood for.

Tony Woodley
Joint General Secretary

* * *

Teacher and Researcher

Bill Silburn was Ken Coates' close colleague at Nottingham University's celebrated Department of Adult Education.

Ken Coates was a good friend of mine for more than 50 years. We first met in 1958 as undergraduates at the University of Nottingham and, between 1966 and the mid-1980s, collaborated on a sequence of teaching and research projects based in that University's Adult Education Department.

The published obituaries that I have seen have understandably concentrated on Ken's political activities, and his period as a member of the European Parliament. Only passing mention was made of his long career as a teacher; but for more than 40 years he worked, first, as a tutor, later as a lecturer, senior lecturer and, finally, as Special Professor in the University of Nottingham's Department of Adult Education. This was work that he took very seriously and with deep commitment, especially his contributions to the Industrial Day Release programmes that for many years were an important part of that Department's responsibility. He had himself worked for several years as a coal miner and had an especially close link with the miners who for many years took part in these programmes. To his classes he brought deep learning and culture but worn lightly and always with humour; he was both a great demystifier and a debunker.

It is fair to say that within the University there were some for whom an important aim of the industrial release work was to encourage the most able and ambitious of the students to aspire to entry to Ruskin College, and thereafter a career in management. While Ken did not object to students developing in that way (if that was what they wanted to do), he had another vision of men and women returning to their workplaces better equipped to play a more effective role in their trade unions and beyond in the life of the wider community. It is certainly the case that throughout the East Midlands there are many men and women who have made and continue to make a valuable contribution to public life, inspired and encouraged by their contacts with Ken.

He and I started to work together closely in 1966, when he asked me to join him in an attempt to set up a study group to verify locally Peter Townsend's suggestion that during the post-war period poverty had actually increased, an idea that flew in the face of all currently received understanding and common sense. A group of 20 participants was successfully convened and embarked upon an enquiry, surveying a run-down neighbourhood (St Ann's) that was very conveniently reached from the Adult Education Centre, and if there was poverty and deprivation it was likely to be found in precisely such a district.

The outcome of this enquiry was the publication of a report, in 1968, that documented in detail widespread and multiple layers of deprivation. This report attracted considerable local comment (not all of it flattering or encouraging) and sufficient national coverage to lead to Thames Television asking us to help them make a documentary film based upon the report; this was made by Stephen Frears and screened in 1969. Meanwhile, Penguin Books commissioned us to write up the study at book-length, and this was published as *Poverty: the Forgotten Englishmen* in 1970.

The study group went on to complete a parallel study on an outlying council housing estate in Nottingham (this too revealed significant pockets of serious deprivation). In the years that followed different study groups carried out neighbourhood surveys in a Derbyshire pit-village threatened by the closure of the mine, and in a small town on the Nottinghamshire-Derbyshire border.

None of this work was noteworthy for its methodological sophistication. It made little or no contribution to social or political theory. Most of it was of modest and often of short-lived local interest. But I know that Ken was very proud of this body of work, and especially proud of the Penguin book, and this pride tells us something important about Ken himself and what drove him to a lifetime of tireless political engagement.

He felt that the great value of *Poverty: The Forgotten Englishmen*, and one of the reasons for its long shelf-life (its fourth edition is still in print with Spokesman Books) is that it gave a voice to people who usually went unheard, it documented social conditions that usually went unseen, and it directly challenged those who profited from the hardships of others, and those with power and authority who failed to act. Moreover he hoped that readers would recognize that the greatest of the deprivations were not the material ones, the shortage of cash, the squalor of the environment and so on, but the moral ones, the lack of effective choices in life, the deprivation of effective control over one's own life and destiny.

And this gives us a clue as to what made Ken tick. He was driven by a profound sensitivity to social injustice, and to the impoverishment of the lives of those blighted by injustice. He needed to understand how these injustices arose and how they were perpetuated, and he found both explanations and clues for action in academic study and in political theory, understandings that deepened and fuelled his empathy with the poor and deprived. In both his teaching and his writing he never lost sight of the individual man, woman and child on whose behalf he worked. He could always translate an observation about a structural phenomenon into its human terms, and felt simultaneously both its social and personal costs. Among the many influences on his life and thought we must include the libertarian values of Tom Paine, and the common decency of Richard Tawney.

Ken's death is a serious loss to the international labour movement. But for those who knew him personally we remember a charismatic and committed teacher, a deeply cultured and learned scholar, a humourous, generous and family-loving companion, and a compassionate friend and comrade.

Bill Silburn

* * *

Ken Coates was one of the most perceptive minds and eloquent voices of the radical left. From the mid-1960s, for four decades he was a major influence in seeking to renew and give greater coherence to militant left politics. ... He won great respect during his 10 years as an MEP, not least for his work as chairman of the human rights sub-committee and his initiatives for an EU-wide Pensioners' Parliament and Disabled People's

Parliament, and a Convention for Full Employment, bringing together trade unionists and unemployed workers' organisations.
John Palmer, from his obituary in *The Guardian*, **29 June 2010**

* * *

Socialist

Michael Barratt Brown worked closely with Ken Coates since the 1960s. These excerpts are taken from his tribute at the funeral. They are followed by Bruce Kent's appreciation.

Ken Coates was a socialist of enormous influence and talent. He was the founder and chief advocate of so many Left wing causes in Britain and Europe that just to list them hardly does justice to his energy and imagination – the Institute for Workers' Control, the Bertrand Russell Peace Foundation and its Tribunals, the Russell Press, the campaign for European Nuclear Disarmament; the Human Rights Committee, the Pensioners' and Disabled People's Parliaments, and the Full Employment Conventions, which all convened in the European Parliament, as did the Brussels Conferences of the European Network for Peace and Human Rights; the *European Labour Forum* journal and associated publications, *The Spokesman* journal and Spokesman Publishing House. To all these initiatives Ken brought a prodigious memory, massive erudition, a vast historical sense, and a deep love of his fellow men and women. His loss to the Labour Movement is irreparable.

What Ken brought to his leadership of these many movements was not only his knowledge and sympathies, but also a considerable oratorical skill and brilliant English writing, which he displayed respectively in many conferences and in the great number of books and articles which he wrote. Ken was a marvellous correspondent, his letters keeping him in touch with a whole range of people, from the Dalai Lama and Chinese dissidents to Noam Chomsky and John Berger, from trade union leaders in Britain and Ireland to those in Europe and beyond, from politicians in the British Parliament to those in many Parties of the European Parliament. His letters, like all his other writings, had a certain directness and firmness, always tempered by modesty and courtesy. We shall all miss his letters.

Ken's experience as a coal miner and the comrades he met among working miners inspired his teaching of miners who came to Nottingham University for Day Release courses in politics, economics and sociology. This in turn led Ken to the creation of the Institute for Workers' Control (IWC), which brought together in a succession of conferences teachers of industrial relations and trade unionists, including some in leading positions such as Bill Jones and Hugh Scanlon. The IWC won support among Labour politicians, even among cabinet ministers, most particularly Tony Benn, but even others such as Eric Varley, an ex-miner, and John Prescott, a one-time seaman, whose studies of their trade union experience the IWC published. Ken even published Gordon Brown's most radical work, *The Red Paper on Scotland*.

Ken's output of books and other writings was voluminous. He was a great collaborator – in his early study of poverty in St. Ann's in Nottingham with Bill Silburn, in his magisterial history of the Transport and General Workers' Union and Essays on Industrial Democracy with Tony Topham, in his European Recovery Programme and his European Full Employment Appeal with Stuart Holland, in his study of the miners' *Community under Attack* and exposure of Blairism in *The Blair Revelation* with Michael Barratt Brown. Working with Ken was always exciting and corrective. His leadership was inspirational and demanding, as the loyal little team at the BRPF – Ken Fleet, Tony Simpson, Rita Maskery, John Daniels, Tom Woodward, Julia James, Abi Rhodes – would all vouchsafe. What they achieved with Ken will remain as his memorial.

Ken's honesty in all his dealings often made him an awkward customer. He was twice thrown out of the Labour Party, once for disagreeing with Harold Wilson over Viet Nam and then for rejecting the proposed arrangement for electing members of the European Parliament, which destroyed the constituency basis of representation. On neither occasion was he given a hearing to make his case. Long before Blair was elected Prime Minister Ken stated his objections to Blair's invention of New Labour and the rejection of the Labour Party's Clause Four, which advocated social ownership and the best possible means of popular control. In the years of New Labour rule Ken concentrated his fire through *The Spokesman* and other publications on challenging Blair's commitment to the United States war policy in Iraq and Afghanistan, and on exposing the destruction of human lives and abuse of human rights that were involved. It seemed like a wholly negative programme, but it had a positive aim to it, in keeping alive the hope of a different world. Without Ken it will be that much more difficult to build that new world, but we should here and now re-dedicate ourselves to that task.

Michael Barratt Brown

* * *

Comet

Ken was, like his sparring partner Edward Thompson, one of the great prophets of the 20th century. Prophets are traditionally old, hairy, censorious, and short on personal friendships. Ken was none of those things. The twinkle in his eye and his infectious laugh are lasting memories.

I knew nothing of his political past when he burst in on me, like a human comet, in the very early 80s, with the END Appeal. He came to discuss 'Protest and Survive', one of the most powerful polemics I have ever read. Written by Edward, it was promoted and produced by Ken. It woke up a generation and encouraged many imitations – not least the Christian version – 'Profess and Survive'. Out of all this came the European Nuclear Disarmament campaign with its aim of building a united, de-militarised, bloc-free Europe. Here at home, END did much to expand CND's traditional focus on British nuclear weapons. But Ken was not just END. He was The Bertrand Russell Peace Foundation and Spokesman Books as well as being, until 'they' got rid of him, a Labour Member of the European Parliament. *The Spokesman* is a small magazine with a clout above its weight. I used to marvel in each issue at the way so little escaped Ken's attention. Ken always knew what wickedness 'they' had been up to and he was well able to forecast what wickedness 'they' would get up to in the future. For one with bad eyesight little went under his political radar. He was of course more than lucky to have Tamara as his wonderful partner, and the strong support team he had at Nottingham. I will miss him as a good friend and source of advice. But as one who believes that the human spirit does not simply evaporate but, like great art and great music, has its own immortality, Ken somehow, somewhere, will go on pushing us towards a kinder and juster world. And if the Angels are not politically organised, they soon will be.

Bruce Kent

* * *

Ken and I were expelled together from the Labour party in January 1998. Our crime was to oppose Tony Blair for his rightwing policies and his attempt to cleanse the Labour party of socialism and democracy; we were, as Ken said later, 'a little ahead of our time'. In June that year, as president of the EU, Mr Blair was making his final report to the European parliament. He was somewhat discomfited to find that the two final speakers in the debate were Ken and I. Ken caused much amusement among the press when he began his speech: 'I think the outgoing presidency should be called the Blair presidency in honour of a great Englishman. I refer of course to Eric Blair, better known as George Orwell, who described how the Europe of 1984 was governed by a Ministry of Truth in which spin doctors explained how the war being organised by the Ministry of Peace was always going well. The language of this world was called Newspeak. New Labour speaks this language to perfection.'

Hugh Kerr, *The Guardian*, **1 July 2010**

Ken Coates with Jacques Delors and Pauline Green MEP.

The radical intellectual

Some personal reflections

Noam Chomsky

Professor Chomsky kindly gave The Spokesman *permission to publish his talk, which was first given on 8 April 2010 in Madison, Wisconsin, at the Havens Center for the Study of Social Structure and Social Change in the Sociology Department at the University of Wisconsin-Madison. His new book is called* Hopes and Prospects *(Hamish Hamilton, £18.99).*

I don't have to say how pleased and grateful I am for this honour, which also offers an occasion to look back over the years. What comes to mind with particular salience is the earliest years, perhaps because I've been thinking a lot about them lately, for other reasons. They were, of course, formative years for me personally, but I think the significance unfortunately goes beyond.

I'm just old enough to have memories of Hitler's speeches on the radio 75 years ago. I didn't understand the words, but couldn't fail to grasp the menace of the tone and the cheering mobs. The first political article I wrote was in February 1939, right after the fall of Barcelona. I'm sure it was nothing memorable. I can recall a little of it, but much more clearly the mood of fear and foreboding. The article opened with the words: 'Austria falls, Czechoslovakia falls, and now Barcelona falls' – and Spain with it, a few months later. The words have always stayed in my mind, along with the dread, the sense of the dark clouds of fascism gathering over Germany and then Europe and perhaps beyond, a growing force of unimaginable horror. Though no one could foresee the Holocaust, *Kristallnacht* had taken place just a few weeks before and the desperate flight of refugees had been building up for years, many of them unable to believe what was happening.

In those years I also had my first experience with radical intellectuals – though they wouldn't be called 'intellectuals' as the term is standardly used, applying to people with status and privilege who are in a position to reach the public with thoughts about human affairs and concerns. And since privilege confers responsibility, the question always arises as to how they are using that responsibility, topics very much alive in those years in work by Erich Fromm, Russell and Dewey, Orwell, Dwight MacDonald, and others, which I soon came to know. But the radical intellectuals of my childhood were different. They were my working-class relatives in New York, mostly unemployed during the Depression, though one uncle, with a disability, had a newsstand thanks to New Deal measures and so was able to help support much of the family. My parents could, too, in a small way. As Hebrew teachers in Philadelphia, they had that rare gift of employment, so we had a stream of aunts and cousins staying with us periodically.

My New York relatives mostly had limited formal education. My uncle, who ran the newsstand and was an enormous influence on my early life, had never gone beyond fourth grade. But it was one of the most lively intellectual circles I have ever been part of, at least on the periphery as a child. There were constant discussions about the latest performance of the Budapest String Quartet, the controversies between Stekel and Freud, radical politics and activism, which was then reaching impressive peaks. Particularly significant were the sit-down strikes, just a step short of workers taking over factories and radically changing the society – ideas that should be very much alive today.

Along with being a major factor in New Deal measures, the rising labour activism aroused great concern in the business world. Its leading figures warned about 'the hazard facing industrialists [with] the rising political power of the masses', and the need to intensify 'the everlasting battle for the minds of men', and instituted programmes to overcome this threat to order and discipline, put aside during the war, but taken up afterward with extreme dedication and scale. The United States is unusual among industrial societies in its highly class-conscious business community, relentlessly fighting a bitter class war, in earlier years with unusual levels of violence, more recently through massive propaganda offensives.

Some of my relatives were close to the Communist Party, others were bitterly anti-Communist from the left; and some, like my uncle, were anti-Bolshevik, from farther left. Among those close to the Party, while there was ritual obeisance to Russia, I had the feeling that for most the focus was right here: the civil rights and labour movements, welfare reform and badly needed social change. The Party was a force that did not anticipate quick victories, but was always present, ready, persistent, dedicated to moving from temporary defeat to the next struggle, something that we really lack today. It was also connected with a broader movement of workers' education and associations and, not least, an opportunity for my unemployed seamstress aunts to spend a week in the country at an International Ladies Garment Workers' Union resort and other escapes from what should have been a very grim world, though I remember it from my own personal experiences – limited of course – as a time that was full of hope, quite unlike today under circumstances that are objectively much less severe.

By 1941, I was spending as much time as I could in downtown Manhattan, gravitating to another group of radical intellectuals in the small bookstores on 4th Avenue run by anarchist refugees from the Spanish revolution of 1936, or the office of the Anarchist *Freie Arbeiter Stimme* in Union Square nearby. They, too, didn't fit the standard formula for intellectuals. But if by the term we mean people who think seriously about life and society, their problems and possible solutions, against a background of knowledge and understanding, then they were indeed intellectuals, impressive ones. They were quite happy to spend time with a young kid who was fascinated with the 1936 anarchist revolution, which I thought then, and still think, was one of the high points of Western civilization and in some ways a beacon for a better future. I picked up a lot of material that I used 30 years later when writing about the topic, most of it not then in print.

Among the most memorable of these materials is a collection of primary documents about collectivization, published in 1937 by the CNT, the anarcho-syndicalist union that is celebrating its centenary this year. One contribution has resonated in my mind ever since, by peasants of the village of Membrilla. I would like to quote parts of it:

> 'In [the] miserable huts [of Membrilla] live the poor inhabitants of a poor province; eight thousand people, but the streets are not paved, the town has no newspaper, no cinema, neither a café nor a library ... Food, clothing and tools were distributed equitably to the whole population. Money was abolished, work collectivized, all goods passed to the community, consumption was socialized. It was, however, not a socialization of wealth but of poverty ... The whole population lived as in a large family; functionaries, delegates, the secretary of the syndicates, the members of the municipal council, all elected, acted as heads of a family. But they were controlled, because special privilege or corruption would not be tolerated. Membrilla is perhaps the poorest village of Spain, but it is the most just.'

These words, by some of the most impoverished peasants in the country, capture with rare eloquence the achievements and promise of the anarchist revolution. The achievements did not, of course, spring up from nothing. They were the outcome of many decades of struggle, experiment, brutal repression – and learning. The concept of how a just society should be organized was in the minds of the population when the opportunity arose.

The experiment in creating a world of freedom and justice was crushed all too soon by the combined forces of fascism, Stalinism and liberal democracy. Global power centres understood very well that they must unite to destroy this dangerous threat to subordination and discipline before turning to the secondary task of dividing up the spoils.

In later years, I have sometimes been able to see first-hand at least a little of the lives of poor people suffering brutal repression and violence – in the miserable slums of Haiti at the peak of the terror in the early 1990s, supported by Washington though the facts are still suppressed and highly relevant to today's tragedies. Or in refugee camps in Laos, where tens of thousands of people were huddled, driven from their homes by a CIA mercenary army after years of trying to survive in caves under relentless bombing that had nothing to do with the war in Vietnam, one of the gravest atrocities of modern history, still largely unknown and still killing many people because the land is saturated with unexploded ordnance. Or in Palestine and south-eastern Turkey and many other places. Among them, particularly important to me for personal reasons, is southern Colombia, where *campesinos*, indigenous people and Afro-Colombians are being driven from their devastated lands by terror and chemical warfare, called here 'fumigation', as if we somehow have the right to destroy other countries on pretexts that we manufacture – people capable of the most miraculous sympathy and humanity, despite the awful suffering in which we play a major role, while looking the other way – though not in Madison, thanks to the work of the Colombia support group here.

One of the things I learned in the anarchist bookstores and offices 70 years ago was that I had been wrong in taking the fall of Barcelona in 1939 to be the death knell for freedom in Spain. It rang two years earlier, in May 1937, when the industrial working class was crushed by the Communist-led repression and Communist armies swept through the countryside destroying the collectives, with the assistance of the liberal democracies and with Hitler and Mussolini waiting in the wings – an immense tragedy for Spain, even though not quite the victory that the predators had anticipated.

A few years later, I left home for graduate studies at Harvard, where I had my first extensive experience with the élite intellectual world. On arrival, I went to the standard faculty-run party for incoming students and was regaled by a very distinguished philosopher with an account of the Depression – which, he assured me, had not taken place. It was a liberal fabrication. There were no rag-pickers coming to our door in desperation in the early 1930s, no women workers being beaten by security forces while on strike at a textile factory that I passed on a trolley with my mother when I was about five, none of my unemployed working class relatives. A few businessmen might have suffered, but there was nothing beyond that.

I was soon to learn that this was far from an exception, but I don't want to suggest that this was typical of Harvard intellectuals. Most were Stevenson liberals, people who applauded when Stevenson said at the UN that we have to defend Vietnam from 'internal aggression', from the 'assault from within', as President Kennedy put it. Words that we hear again today, for example, last Sunday, in *The New York Times*, where we read that after the conquest of Marja in Helmand Province, the Marines have collided with a Taliban identity so dominant that the movement appears more akin to the only political organization in a one-party town, with an influence that touches everyone. 'We've got to re-evaluate our definition of the word "enemy",' said Brig. Gen. Larry Nicholson, commander of the Marine expeditionary brigade in Helmand Province. 'Most people here identify themselves as Taliban … We have to readjust our thinking so we're not trying to chase the Taliban out of Marja, we're trying to chase the enemy out,' he said.

A problem that has always bedeviled conquerors, very familiar to the United States from Vietnam, where the leading US government scholar in a widely praised book lamented that the enemy within was the only 'truly mass-based political party in South Vietnam' and any effort of ours to compete with it politically would be like a conflict between a minnow and a whale, so we had to overcome their political force by using our comparative advantage, violence – as we did. Others have faced similar problems: for example, the Russians in Afghanistan in the 1980s, an invasion that also elicited the outrage that we muster up for the crimes of enemies. Middle East specialist William Polk reminds us that the Russians 'won many military victories and through their civic action programs they actually won over many of the villages' – and in fact, as we know from reliable sources, created substantial freedom in Kabul, particularly for women. But, to go on with Polk, 'over the decade of their involvement, the Russians won almost every battle and occupied at one time or another virtually every inch of the country, but they lost … the war. When they gave up and left, the Afghans resumed their traditional way of life.'

The dilemmas faced by Obama and McChrystal are not quite the same. The enemy whom the Marines are trying to chase out of their villages have virtually no outside support. The Russian invaders, in sharp contrast, were facing a resistance that received vital support from the US, Saudi Arabia and Pakistan, who were rounding up the most extreme radical Islamic fundamentalists they could find – including those terrorizing women in

Kabul – and were arming them with advanced weapons, while also carrying forward the programme of radical Islamization of Pakistan, yet another one of Reagan's gifts to the world, along with Pakistan's nuclear weapons. The goal of these US operations was not to defend Afghanistan. It was explained frankly by the CIA station chief in Islamabad, who was running the operations. The goal was to 'kill Soviet Soldiers'. He boasted that he 'loved' this 'noble goal', making it very clear, in his words, that 'the mission was not to liberate Afghanistan', which he didn't care about. You're familiar I'm sure with Zbigniew Brzezinski's somewhat similar boasts.

By the early 1960s, I was deeply engaged in antiwar activities. I won't go into the details, though they tell us a lot about the intellectual climate, particularly in liberal Boston. By 1966, my own involvement was deep enough so that my wife went back to college to get a degree after 17 years because of the likelihood of a long prison sentence – which came very close. The trial was already announced, but cancelled after the Tet offensive, which convinced the business community that the war was becoming too costly and, in any event, the major war aims had been achieved – another long story I won't go into. After the Tet offensive and the shift in official policy, it suddenly turned out that everyone had been a long-term opponent of the war – in deep silence. Kennedy memoirists rewrote their accounts to present their hero as a dove – untroubled by the radical revisions or by the extensive documentary evidence showing that JFK would consider withdrawal from a war he knew to be domestically unpopular only after victory was assured.

Even before the Tet offensive there were growing doubts in these circles, not about the sentimental notions of right and wrong that we reserve for the crimes of enemies, but about the likelihood of success in beating back the 'assault from within'. Perhaps, a paradigm was Arthur Schlesinger's reflections when he was beginning to be concerned that victory might not be so easily at hand. As he put it, 'we all pray' that the hawks will be right and that the surge of the day will bring victory. And if it does, we will be praising the 'wisdom and statesmanship' of the US government in gaining military victory while leaving 'the tragic country gutted and devastated by bombs, burned by napalm, turned into a wasteland by chemical defoliation, a land of ruin and wreck', with its 'political and institutional fabric' pulverized. But escalation probably won't succeed and will prove to be too costly for ourselves, so perhaps strategy should be rethought.

Little has changed today when Obama is hailed as a leading opponent of the Iraq invasion because it was a 'strategic blunder', words that one could also have read in *Pravda* by the mid-1980s. The imperial mentality is very deeply rooted.

It is sad to say, but not false, that within the dominant spectrum the liberal imperialists are 'the good guys'. A likely alternative is revealed by the most recent polls. Almost half of voters say that the average Tea Party member is closer to their views than President Obama, whom fewer prefer. There's an interesting breakdown. Eighty-seven per cent of those in the so-called 'Political Class' say their views are closer to Obama's. Sixty-three per cent of what are called 'Mainstream Americans' say their views are closer to the Tea Party. On virtually all issues, Republicans are trusted by the electorate more than Democrats, in many cases by double digits. Other evidence suggests that these polls are recording distrust rather than trust. The level of anger and fear in the country is like nothing I can recall in my lifetime. And since the Democrats are in power, the revulsion over the current social-economic-political world attaches to them.

Unfortunately, these attitudes are understandable. For over 30 years, real incomes for the majority of the population have stagnated or declined, social indicators have steadily deteriorated since the mid-1970s after closely tracking growth in earlier years, work hours and insecurity have increased along with debt. Wealth has accumulated, but into very few pockets, leading to probably record inequality. These are, in large part, consequences of the financialization of the economy since the 1970s and the corresponding hollowing out of domestic production. What people see before their eyes is that the bankers who are primarily responsible for the current crisis and who were saved from bankruptcy by the public are now revelling in record profits and huge bonuses, while official unemployment stays at about 10 per cent and in manufacturing is at depression levels, one in six, with good jobs unlikely to return. People rightly want answers and they are not getting them, except from voices that tell tales that have some internal coherence, but only if you suspend disbelief and enter into their world of irrationality and deceit. Ridiculing Tea Party shenanigans is a serious error, I think. It would be far more appropriate to understand what lies behind them and to ask ourselves why justly angry people are being mobilized by the extreme right and not by forces like those that did so in my childhood, in the days of formation of the Congress of Industrial Organizations (CIO) and other constructive activism.

To take just one illustration of the operation of really existing market democracy, Obama's primary constituency was financial institutions, which have gained such dominance in the economy that their share of corporate profits rose from a few per cent in the 1970s to almost one-third today. They preferred Obama to McCain and largely bought the election for him. They expected to be rewarded and were. But a few months ago, responding to rising public anger, Obama began to criticize the 'greedy bankers' who had been rescued by the public and even proposed some measures to constrain them. Punishment for his deviation was swift. The major banks announced prominently that they would shift funding to Republicans if Obama persisted with his offensive rhetoric.

Obama heard the message. Within days, he informed the business press that bankers are fine 'guys'. He singled out for special praise the chairs of two leading beneficiaries of public largess, JP Morgan Chase and Goldman Sachs and assured the business world that, 'I, like most of the American people, don't begrudge people success or wealth' – such as the bonuses and profits that are infuriating the public. 'That's part of the free market system,' Obama continued, not inaccurately, as the concept 'free market' is interpreted in state capitalist doctrine.

This should not be a great surprise. That incorrigible radical Adam Smith, speaking of England, observed that the principal architects of power were the owners of the society, in his day the merchants and manufacturers, and they made sure that policy would attend scrupulously to their interests, however 'grievous' the impact on the people of England, and, worse, the victims of 'the savage injustice of the Europeans' abroad. British crimes in India were a primary concern of an old-fashioned conservative with moral values, a category that a Diogenes might search for today.

A modern and more sophisticated version of Smith's maxim is political economist Thomas Ferguson's 'investment theory of politics', which takes elections to be occasions when groups of investors coalesce to invest to control the state by selecting the architects of policies who will serve their interests. It turns out to be a very good predictor of policy over long periods. That should hardly be surprising. Concentrations of economic power will naturally seek to extend their sway over any political process. It happens to be extreme in the United States, as I mentioned.

There is much fevered discussion these days about whether, or when, the United States is going to lose its dominant position in global affairs to China and India, the rising world powers. There is an element of truth to these laments. But apart from misconceptions about debt, deficits and the actual state of China and India, the discussions are based on a serious misconception of the nature of power and its exercise. In scholarship and public discourse, it is common to take the actors in international affairs to be states that pursue some mysterious goal called 'the national interest', divorced from the internal distribution of power. Adam Smith had a sharper eye and his radical truism provides a useful corrective. Bearing it in mind, we can see that there is indeed a global shift of power, though not the one that occupies centre stage: a further shift from the global workforce to transnational capital, sharply escalating during the neoliberal years. The cost is substantial, including working people in the United States, starving peasants in India and millions of protesting workers in China, where labour share in national income is declining even more rapidly than in most of the world.

Political economist Martin Hart-Landsberg observes that China does play a leading role in the real global shift of power, having become largely an assembly plant for a regional production system. Japan, Taiwan, and other advanced Asian economies export parts and components to China and provide most of the sophisticated technology. Chinese labour assembles it and exports it. To illustrate, a Sloan Foundation study estimated that for a $150 iPod exported from China, about 3 percent of value added is by China, but it is counted as a Chinese export. Much concern has been aroused by the growing US trade deficit with China, but less noticed is the fact that the trade deficit with Japan and rest of Asia has sharply declined as the new regional production system takes shape. A *Wall Street Journal* report concluded that if value added were properly calculated, the real US-China trade deficit would decline by as much as 30 per cent, while the US trade deficit with Japan would rise by 25 per cent. US manufacturers are following the same course, providing parts and components for China to assemble and export, mostly back to the United States. For the financial institutions, retail giants, ownership and management of manufacturing industries and sectors closely related to this nexus of power, all of this is heavenly. Not for American workers, but as Smith pointed out, their fate is not the concern of the 'principal architects of policy'.

It's true that there is nothing fundamentally new in the process of deindustrialization. Owners and managers naturally seek the lowest labour costs; efforts to do otherwise, famously by Henry Ford, were struck down by the courts, so now it is a legal obligation. One means is shifting production. In earlier days, the shift was mostly internal, especially to the southern states, where labour could be more harshly repressed. Major corporations, like the US steel corporation of the sainted philanthropist Andrew Carnegie, could also profit from the new slave-labour force created by the criminalization of black life after the end of Reconstruction in 1877, a core component of the American industrial revolution, continuing until World War Two. It is being reproduced in part during the recent neoliberal period, with the drug war used as a pretext to drive the superfluous population, mostly black, back to the prisons, also providing a new supply of prison labour in state or private prisons, much of it in violation of international labour conventions. For many African-Americans, since they were exported to the colonies, life has scarcely escaped the bonds of slavery, or sometimes worse. More recently the shift is mostly abroad.

Returning to the charges against 'greedy bankers', in fairness, we should concede that they have a valid defence. Their task is to maximize profit and market share; in fact, that's their legal obligation. If they don't do it, they'll be replaced by someone who will. These are institutional facts, as are the inherent market inefficiencies that require them to ignore systemic risk: the likelihood that transactions they enter into will harm the economy generally. They know full well that these policies are likely to tank the economy, but these externalities, as they are called, are not their business, and cannot be, not because they are bad people, but for institutional reasons. It is also unfair to accuse them of 'irrational exuberance', to borrow Alan Greenspan's brief recognition of reality during the artificial tech boom of the late 1990s. Their exuberance and risk taking was quite rational, in the knowledge that when it all collapses, they can flee to the shelter of the nanny state, clutching their copies of Hayek, Friedman and Rand. The government insurance policy is one of many perverse incentives that magnify the inherent market inefficiencies.

In brief, ignoring systemic risk is an inherent institutional property and perverse incentives are an application of Smith's maxim. Again, no great insight.

After the latest disaster occurred, it has been agreed by leading economists that an 'emerging consensus' has developed 'on the need for macroprudential supervision' of financial markets, that is, 'paying attention to the stability of the financial system as a whole and not just its individual parts' (Barry Eichengreen, one of the most respected analysts and historians of the financial system). Two prominent international economists add that, 'There is growing recognition that our financial system is running a doomsday cycle'. Whenever it fails, we rely on lax money and fiscal policies to bail it out. This response teaches the financial sector: take large gambles to get paid handsomely and don't worry about the costs – they will be paid by taxpayers through bailouts and other devices and the financial system 'is thus resurrected to gamble again – and to fail again'. The system is a 'doom loop', in the words of the official of the Bank of England responsible for financial stability.

Basically the same logic applies elsewhere. A year ago, the business world recognized that the insurance companies and big Pharma, in sharp defiance of the public will, had succeeded in destroying the possibility of serious health reform – a very serious matter, not only for the people who suffer from the dysfunctional health system, but even on narrow economic grounds. About half of the deficit that we are instructed to deplore is attributable to unprecedented military expenditures, rising under Obama, and most of the rest to the increasing costs of the virtually unregulated privatized health care system, unique in the industrial world, also unique in its gifts to drug companies – opposed by a mere 85 per cent of the population. Last August, *Business Week* had a cover story celebrating the victory of the health insurance industries. Of course, no victory is enough, so they persisted in the struggle, gaining more, also against the will of the large majority of the public, another interesting story I'll have to put aside.

Observing this victory, the American Petroleum Institute, backed by the Chamber of Commerce and the other great business lobbies, announced that they are going to use the model of the health industry campaigns to intensify their massive propaganda efforts to convince the public to dismiss concerns about anthropogenic global warming. That has been done with great success; those who believe in this liberal hoax have reduced to barely a third of the population. The executives dedicated to this task know as well as the rest of us that the liberal hoax is real and the prospects grim. But they are fulfilling their institutional role. The fate of the species is an externality that they must ignore, to the extent that market systems prevail.

One of the clearest and most moving articulations of the public mood that I have seen was written by Joseph Andrew Stack, who crashed his small plane into an office building in Austin, Texas, a few weeks ago, committing suicide. He left a manifesto explaining his actions. It was mostly ridiculed, but it deserves much better, I think.

Stack's manifesto traces the life history that led him to this final desperate act. The story begins when he was a teenage student living on a pittance in Harrisburg, Pennsylvania, near the heart of what was once a great industrial centre. His neighbour was a woman in her 80s, surviving on cat food, the 'widowed wife of a retired steel worker. Her husband had worked all his life in the steel mills of central Pennsylvania with promises from big business and the union that, for his 30 years of service, he would have a pension and medical care to look forward to in his retirement. Instead he was one of the thousands who got nothing because the incompetent mill management and corrupt union (not to mention the government) raided their pension funds and stole their retirement. All she had was social security to live on' (quoting); and Stack could have added that there have been concerted and continuing efforts by the super rich and their political allies to take even that away on spurious grounds. Stack decided then that he couldn't trust big business and would strike out on his own, only to discover that he couldn't trust a government that cared nothing about people like him, but only about the rich and privileged, or a legal system in which, in his words, 'there are two "interpretations" for every law, one for the very rich and one for the rest of us'. Or a government that leaves us with 'the joke we call the American medical system, including the drug and insurance companies [that] are murdering tens of thousands of people a year', with care rationed largely by wealth, not need. All in a social order in which 'a handful of thugs and plunderers can commit unthinkable atrocities … and when it's time for their gravy train to crash under the weight of their gluttony and overwhelming stupidity, the force of the full federal government has no difficulty coming to their aid within days if not hours'. And much more.

Stack tells us that his desperate final act was an effort to show that there are people willing to die for their freedom, in the hope of awakening others from their torpor. It wouldn't surprise me if he had in mind the premature death of the steel worker that taught him about the real world as a teenager. That steel worker didn't literally commit suicide after having been discarded to the trash heap, but it's far from an isolated case; we can add his and many similar cases to the colossal toll of the institutional crimes of state capitalism.

There are poignant studies of the indignation and rage of those who have been cast aside as the state-corporate programmes of financialization and deindustrialization have closed plants and destroyed families and communities. They reveal the sense of acute betrayal on the part of working people who believed they had fulfilled their duty to society in a moral compact with business and government, only to discover that they had been only instruments for profit and power, truisms from which they had been carefully protected by doctrinal institutions.

Reading Joe Stack's manifesto and a great deal more like it, I find myself recovering childhood memories and much more that I did not then understand. The Weimar Republic was the peak of western civilization in the sciences and the arts, also regarded as a model of democracy. Through the 1920s, the traditional liberal and conservative parties entered into inexorable decline, well before the process was intensified by the Great Depression. The coalition that elected General Hindenburg in 1925 was not very different from the mass base that swept Hitler into office eight years later, compelling the aristocratic Hindenburg to select as chancellor the 'little corporal' he despised. As late as 1928, the Nazis had less than 3 per cent of the vote. Two years later, the most respectable Berlin press was lamenting the sight of the many millions in this 'highly civilized country' who had 'given their vote to the commonest, hollowest and crudest charlatanism'. The public was becoming disgusted with the incessant wrangling of Weimar politics, the service of the traditional parties to powerful interests and their failure to deal with popular grievances. They were drawn to forces dedicated to upholding the greatness of the nation and defending it against invented threats in a revitalized, armed and unified state, marching to a glorious future, led by the charismatic figure who was carrying out 'the will of eternal Providence, the Creator of the universe', as he orated to the mesmerized masses. By May 1933, the Nazis had largely destroyed not only the traditional ruling parties, but even the huge working-class parties, the Social Democrats and Communists, along with their very powerful associations. The Nazis declared May Day 1933 to be a workers' holiday, something the left parties had never been able to achieve. Many working people took part in the enormous patriotic demonstrations, with more than a million people at the heart of Red Berlin, joining farmers, artisans, shopkeepers, paramilitary forces, Christian organizations, athletic and riflery clubs, and the rest of the coalition that was taking shape as the centre collapsed. By the onset of the war, perhaps 90 per cent of Germans were marching with the brown shirts.

As I mentioned, I am just old enough to remember those chilling and ominous days of Germany's descent from decency to Nazi barbarism, to borrow the words of the distinguished scholar of German history Fritz Stern. He tells us that he has the future of the United States in mind when he reviews 'a historic process in which resentment against a disenchanted secular world found deliverance in the ecstatic escape of unreason'.

The world is too complex for history to repeat, but there are nevertheless lessons to keep in mind. There is no shortage of tasks for those who choose the vocation of critical intellectuals, whatever their station in life. They can seek to sweep away the mists of carefully contrived illusion and reveal the stark reality. They can become directly engaged in popular struggles, helping to organize the countless Joe Stacks who are destroying themselves and maybe the world and to join them in leading the way to a better future.

Copyright 2010 by Noam Chomsky

'A nuclear-weapon-free Europe from Poland to Portugal' – surrounding the International Congress Centre, Berlin, where the second END convention met in 1983.

'Maybe we should talk about my books'

Henning Mankell

The bestselling Swedish crime writer Henning Mankell, whose detective novels featuring Kurt Wallander have sold almost 30 million copies worldwide, was aboard the Swedish ship Sofia, *one of six ships in the flotilla carrying aid to Gaza. On 31 May, the 25-strong crew, including Mankell, were kidnapped on the high seas and taken to Israel where they were held in custody. A few days later, following his deportation from Israel, Mr Mankell told a press conference in Berlin of his experiences. We print short excerpts.*

'I am against the politics of Israel today because that is a sort of an apartheid. I was against that sort of politics in South Africa, and I am against it now.'

* * *

'… It was an act of sea piracy when they attacked the boat, when they took the boat to Israel, we were actually kidnapped … Of course, I am not an anti-semite. I must maybe say that I was in Israel, in Palestine, just one month ago. I was part of a Palestinian literary festival – I visited Hebron and Ramallah. I was also there last year, and I can assure you that every time I go to Israel I meet more and more Israeli activists. That says to me that the situation now is horrifying. It can't continue. They also participate in trying to find ways that solidarity can work to find a solution to all the problems. And I guess this is growing day to day as more and more people understand the need to discontinue this unbearable situation.

I discuss with all my Jewish friends in Europe who are very worried about what is happening. I can tell you – I would say it is funny but there is nothing funny about this – but when I had been taken to Israel I was put in front of, I don't know whether he was a policeman or whether he was a judge. I don't know because they don't tell you their names. I had this man from the foreign department to stay by my side and that man said to me … I asked him "what am I charged with?"

He said, "you are charged with entering Israel illegally".

I said, "this is absolutely absurd. How can I be charged with this when you brought me here. I didn't want to come."

And then he didn't want to discuss anymore, and I said, "please, I want to discuss more with you," and then he started to talk about something else.

He said, "I know who you are and I read your books and I like them."

"Oh that's nice," I said. "OK, maybe we should talk about my books then if you don't want to talk about the charges."

"No, I don't want to do that, but maybe I sometimes go to Europe."

Then I say, "OK, I will give you my telephone number in Sweden so next time you go to Sweden, if you let me out, if you don't send me to prison, let's talk about what is happening here."

He looked at me. "Do you mean that?"

"Yes," then I looked up my phone number and gave it to him. After that I was sent away to be deported.

But I think I tried to talk with him because I believe in the rational mind. There must be a solution. Of course the Jewish people have to be a very important part of that solution. I try to listen and I try to talk to people.'

* * *

'In a way I am sad that now I know that I will not be able to go back to Jerusalem because they won't let me in. But this is maybe the price one has to pay.'

Solidarity with the people of Palestine

Lift the blockade now!

Bob Crow
General Secretary

Alex Gordon
President

What the spooks want

Tony Simpson

Britain now has a National Security Council, headed by Sir Peter Ricketts, a Foreign Office civil servant. He it was who advised Jack Straw, in March 2002, that 'the truth is that what has changed is not the pace of Saddam Hussein's weapons of mass destruction programmes, but our tolerance of them post-11 September'. Straw duly repeated this sage judgment to the Prime Minister, but Mr Blair wasn't minded to heed the caution implicit in Sir Peter's words. The Prime Minister was off to Crawford, Texas, where President Bush would apprise him of the current state of US planning for the war on Iraq. Blair joined in the President's warmongering against Iraq, with all the deceptions and distortions that entailed.

Such a baleful experience may have contributed to the motivation, which seems to have been felt latterly within the British Establishment, and has sometimes been on display at the Chilcot Inquiry, to regularise governmental discussions of peace and war as well as related matters usually lumped under the catch-all heading of 'security'. 'Sofa' government, that hallmark of the Blair years, had attended British complicity in all the horrors of the clandestine 'war on terror' which was being waged by President Bush's torturers, closely assisted by the lawyers of the Office of Legal Counsel (see *Spokesman 104*).

It was Sir Richard Dearlove, formerly head of the Secret Intelligence Service, whose spies range across the globe, who was one of the first to propose publicly a National Security Council for Britain. Speaking at Gresham College in the City of London in November 2009, he said:

The author is assistant editor of The Spokesman.

'I firmly recommend and support the idea of creating a National Security Council, chaired by the Prime Minister, which meets regularly and can pull together the various ministers and officials relevant to the creation of policy, and, if necessary, can take direct control of a crisis.

I also think we should create the post of a National Security Adviser, with supporting staff, to give the Council a permanent expression and to do some of the longer term conceptual thinking and planning. This is following quite closely the American model, but I would advocate a much lighter bureaucracy here than exists in the States to support their National Security Council.'

Sir Richard seems, at least, to have made some progress on this first part of his agenda. Indeed, the new National Security Council met on day one of the new government, with both Cameron and Clegg attending. This was even before the new Cabinet had had a chance to meet. According to reports, the Council discussed Afghanistan, although 'Afpak' might have been a more accurate description, as we shall see later.

But, first of all, we might consider Sir Richard's wider ambitions for Britain's spooks. He went on to tell Gresham College:

'I think we should create a National Security Staff College which would train around a cohesive programme all the senior staff of the intelligence and security agencies and make them more interchangeable. It might also put an end to the anomaly of unqualified senior officials being parachuted into senior national security appointments. It would also embrace selected law enforcement officers, armed forces officers, and other civil servants, as appropriate, to create a cohesive, cross-Government, national security culture.'

There's no mention of this in the coalition agreement published by the Conservatives and Liberal Democrats. However, having got their Council, who's to say that, notwithstanding our cash-strapped times, the Establishment won't get its Security Staff College for advanced studies in spookery? Sir Richard sets an exacting standard for the new College:

'... it should also aim to be the centre of European excellence in national security. I think it is far more effective for the UK to train Europe's national security experts in a field in which the UK is clearly pre-eminent, rather than try to create another European institution at 27 in Brussels to deal with this. In my practice, they do not really deliver what you want, particularly in such sensitive areas.'

That should go down well elsewhere in Europe. Now that the City has lost some of its allure, Britain can trade on top-of-the-range spooks. Sir Richard, however, downplays his ambitions:

'These may sound like modest changes, but I think that, over time, their impact could be far-reaching in creating greater consensus about what really constitutes our national security concerns in strengthening the Government's structures to deliver policy and strengthen the cadre of professionals, both in the UK and Europe, who would lead the delivery.'

This is quite a far-reaching project. We are witnessing the early stages of its public appearance. What might have been said when its inaugural meeting considered Afghanistan. Once again, Sir Richard can probably help us. He told Gresham College:

> 'the irony of this evening's talk is that, in talking about the UK's national security, I have spoken much more about Pakistan. Of course I have done this deliberately to try to bring home to you just how much we are now part of an interdependent security regime, how we cannot really stand apart from problems which we might prefer to regard as distant and alien. As I said, the line between what is domestic and what is foreign has disappeared, and in conclusion, I would say effective national security has no frontiers any longer.'

Why is Pakistan so important? Sir Richard can help us once again:

> 'The Obama Administration, in my view, is right to speak of AfPak. Our own [Brown] Government could talk more of Pakistan when it talks of Afghanistan, and the dangers to international security were Pakistan to be threatened with disintegration, particularly – and this is an important point – if the integrity of its nuclear arsenal were also in question. For me, the stability of Pakistan is just as important as taking on Al Qaeda, and actually, taking a medium to long term view, I think Pakistan's stability is really the stronger reason for not leaving Afghanistan prematurely.'

Perhaps that is what is now being chewed over at the National Security Council. Shouldn't we be told?

* * *

Afghanistan – 'We're losing'

General Stanley McChrystal's sudden removal, in late June 2010, as US and Nato commander in Afghanistan caused consternation in military circles. One senior British soldier said at the time, 'You just couldn't make this up. Our assumption was that Obama wouldn't move McChrystal because of the disruption it would cause at the top of Nato. But we were proved wrong.' Now the growing disarray in Afghanistan has burst into public view.

President Obama had appointed McChrystal to take charge in Afghanistan in March 2009, shortly after entering office. The General's task was to 'to disrupt, dismantle and defeat Al Qaeda in Pakistan and Afghanistan'. To assist him in this, an additional 21,000 US troops were to be sent to Kabul, the largest increase since the war began in 2001. But the General and his Commander in Chief didn't hit it off. One of McChrystal's staff told the journalist Michael Hastings, whose article for *Rolling Stone* magazine triggered the General's departure,

> 'their first one-on-one meeting took place in the Oval Office ... Obama clearly didn't know anything about him, who he was. Here's the guy who's going to run his fucking war, but he didn't seem very engaged. The Boss was pretty disappointed.'

Notwithstanding the poor personal chemistry with the President, Hastings tells us, McChrystal was determined to use Afghanistan 'as a laboratory for a controversial military strategy known as counter-insurgency or COIN'. So why did he have to go?

Certainly, some of McChrystal's staff, which includes a former head of UK special forces, are highly critical of members of Obama's Administration. Vice President Joe Biden was the butt of numerous jokes. Obama's National Security Advisor, General Jim Jones, was called a 'clown ... stuck in 1985'. General McChrystal himself reportedly has strong reservations about Richard Holbrooke, the President's Special Representative for Afghanistan and Pakistan. Apparently, McChrystal thinks Holbrooke is like 'a wounded animal' who 'keeps hearing rumours that he's going to get fired'! But Hillary Clinton is rated because she supported McChrystal during the strategic review of policy in Afghanistan.

And why is McChrystal's departure felt so acutely in Afghanistan? One key reason is that McChrystal, not Holbrooke nor Karl Eikenberry, US Ambassador to Afghanistan, was closest to President Karzai. He tried hard to help Karzai fashion some vestige of credibility with his own people so that his counter-insurgency strategy might have a national leader to give it support. But now the US Administration must start again. Obama has turned to General Petraeus, instigator of the 'surge' in Iraq, for assistance. Whether relations with him can survive longer than those with McChrystal remains to be seen.

But the real damage done by General McChrystal, rather surprisingly, has been to US Army morale. He had been held in high esteem by ordinary soldiers. A British officer in Kabul said the lads

> 'love Stan McChrystal. You'd be out in Somewhere, Iraq, and someone would take a knee beside you, and a corporal would be like "Who the fuck is that?" And it's fucking Stan McChrystal.'

All that was changing, even before the General was dumped. *Rolling Stone* visited troops on the frontline in Afghanistan. Their correspondent sent back reports of deep misgivings about how the US was losing its war in Afghanistan. The President may have been sold on counter-insurgency but, as Hastings observes, many of McChrystal's 'own men aren't buying it'.

In an attempt to kill fewer civilians, soldiers had been issued with new regulations which say 'Patrol only in areas that you are reasonably certain that you will not have to defend yourselves with lethal force'.

> 'Does that make any fucking sense?' asks Private First Class Jared Pautsch. 'We should just drop a fucking bomb on this place. You sit and ask yourself: What are we doing here?'

Another veteran of three combat tours says of McChrystal's leadership

> 'by the time his directives get passed down to us through Big Army, they're all fucked up – either because somebody is trying to cover their ass, or because they just don't understand it themselves. But we're fucking losing this thing.'

General McChrystal and his team may have given offence in the Oval Office and beyond, but surely their gravest mistake was to create a situation which let a little light shine on what the ordinary Joe on the frontline in Afghanistan really thinks. It was ten years before the Soviet Union eventually withdrew, in 1989, from that country. Will the United States, the UK and Nato take even longer?

COMMUNICATION WORKERS UNION

NATO troops out of Afghanistan

Billy Hayes
General Secretary

Davie Bowman
President

'Nonsense' about Afghanistan

Richard Barrett heads a UN team tracking the Taliban and al-Qaeda. Formerly, he was in charge of counter-terrorism at Britain's Secret Intelligence Service. On 14 June, the Financial Times *published his candid remarks about western policy in Afghanistan and the false claims made for it.*

' ... Putting more troops in is in danger of making things worse ... If you push troops into these areas, then clearly they are no longer going to be quiet ... This idea that they can clear up Kandahar, take control of Kandahar, and that would really weaken the Taliban, I think it's mistaken ... The US cannot be seen to lose a big, well advertised operation as planned for Kandahar. It would be very difficult to recover from such a setback ... It's altogether on a different scale from Marjah. General McChrystal has to make the objectives achievable without looking as if he has already retreated from his original plan because it was beyond him. I think he got a bit carried away and over-optimistic, ambitious.'

Mr Barrett noted that Hamid Karzai, the Afghan president, had been 'notably lukewarm about the whole Kandahar thing'.

'I don't think western states have a clear policy; they don't know, they just don't know, what to do,' he said.

Mr Barrett dismissed the argument advanced by British ministers that the presence of 9,500 British troops in Afghanistan would reduce the threat to the UK.

'That's complete rubbish. I've never heard such nonsense,' he said, warning that the presence of foreign troops risked inflaming anti-western sentiment among British Muslim communities. 'I'm quite sure if there were no foreign troops in Afghanistan there'd be less agitation in Leeds, or wherever, about Pakistanis extremely upset, or suspicious about what western intentions are in Afghanistan and Pakistan.'

Mr Barrett also warned that the Taliban did not appear inclined to respond to overtures made by Mr Karzai at a three-day peace meeting in Kabul two weeks earlier. 'There are huge ... hurdles to overcome before you can get any sort of effective reconciliation ... They're not going to negotiate from a position of weakness ... They're more likely to negotiate, I think, from a position of strength, when they feel they can get a really good deal ... But we've got to be clear on what do they want, and I'm not even sure that we know what the Taliban really want.'

David Kelly – A fresh inquiry into his death?

It is six years since Dr David Kelly died, but the controversy surrounding Lord Hutton's finding of suicide goes on. There is no credible evidence that he killed himself. In Spokesman 107 *we published the transcript of a radio interview given by Dr David Halpin, one of six experienced doctors who want a proper inquest into Dr Kelly's death. 'We do not believe you can bleed to death from the matchstick thin ulnar artery being cut across in his left wrist,' said Dr Halpin. Now, the new Justice Minister, Kenneth Clarke, is reconsidering the case, as the BBC reported on 11 June.*

'Justice Secretary Ken Clarke is considering releasing medical documents on the death of Dr David Kelly to a group of doctors demanding an inquest, the BBC understands. The doctors have questioned Lord Hutton's 2004 verdict of suicide on the government weapons scientist. They have been calling for material from the post-mortem to be released. Lord Hutton requested a 70-year gagging order on it but has said he does not object to the doctors seeing it. He said in January that the purpose of the secrecy order, made at the conclusion of his inquiry, had been to avoid causing distress to Dr Kelly's family. He wrote to ministers in the previous Labour government to say that the report may be seen by the doctors.

Now Ken Clarke is considering whether to release the material. In a statement, the Ministry of Justice said: "The Secretary of State will consider the full facts surrounding this issue."

Mr Clarke could decide to launch a public inquiry into Dr Kelly's death and it is understood conversations have taken place between ministers in the new coalition government, including Attorney General Dominic Grieve, about such a possibility. When the Conservatives were in opposition, Mr Grieve backed calls for the investigation into Dr Kelly's death to be re-opened as the public "have not been reassured" by the official verdict that he killed himself. He also praised the campaigning doctors who questioned Hutton's verdict for making a "cogent" case. As the most senior law officer in England and Wales, he could now ask the High Court to reopen the inquest into the scientist's death. Mr Grieve is not actively pursuing this course of action at the moment but it is thought he would do so if he was persuaded there was fresh evidence.

Transport Minister Norman Baker, a Lib Dem MP who has carried out his own investigation into Dr Kelly's death, is also reported to have been pushing government colleagues for a fresh inquiry.

Dr Kelly's body was found in woods close to his Oxfordshire home in 2003, shortly after it was revealed that he was the source of a BBC report casting doubt on the government's claim that Iraq had weapons of mass destruction capable of being fired within 45 minutes. An inquest was suspended by then Lord Chancellor Lord Falconer, who ruled that Lord Hutton's inquiry could take its place. Lord Hutton's report in 2004 concluded that Dr Kelly had killed himself by cutting an artery in his wrist. But the campaigning doctors claim there was insufficient evidence to prove beyond reasonable doubt he killed himself.

The experts include trauma surgeon David Halpin, epidemiologist Andrew Rouse, surgeon Martin Birnstingl, former assistant coroner Dr Michael Powers QC, radiologist Stephen Frost, and Chris Burns-Cox who specialises in internal general medicine.'

Gallows
and Other Tales of Suspicion and Obsession
by *John Arden*

John Arden has produced another glorious collection of stories, set in Yorkshire, London and Ireland. *Gallows* mingles black comedy with melodrama to probe the underside of Irish and English history from the 17th century to the 21st. The title-piece is a ghost story set in contemporary Galway: a nightmare of ghastly slaughter resurfacing from the era of the Penal Laws. Described in *The Guardian* newspaper as 'the British Brecht', John Arden was born in Barnsley. He has lived in Ireland for four decades. He is the author of plays such as *All Fall Down*, which appeared in 1955, *Serjeant Musgrave's Dance* (1959), *Live Like Pigs*, and *The Non-Stop Connolly Show*, co-authored and co-produced in 1975 with Margaretta D'Arcy. Added to all this, there are novels and short stories.

'Hilarious, entertaining, page-turning, fascinating and almost any other quality you might fancy in a damned good read.' Harry Browne, *The Sunday Times*

506 pages | Paperback plus DVD | £24.00 including UK delivery direct from:

Spokesman Books, Russell House, Bulwell Lane, Nottingham, NG6 0BT, UK.
email: elfeuro@compuserve   **fax**: ++44 (0)1159 420433
www.spokesmanbooks.com

Why I am a Guildsman

Bertrand Russell

Russell's statement was published in 1919 in The Guildsman: a Journal of Social and Industrial Freedom, *edited by G.D.H.Cole.*

I have been led to Guild Socialism by the consideration of what seemed to me the good and bad elements in the existing system and in older proposals for reconstruction: it seemed to me that Guild Socialism combined the good elements and avoided those that were bad more successfully than any of its rivals.

The greatest evil of the existing system is, to my mind, the concentration of economic power, the arguments against which are exactly the same as those against the concentration of political power, being, in fact, the familiar arguments in favour of democracy. So long as economic power remains in the hands of a few, democracy is a sham. The evils of poverty and exploitation are glaring, and are, so far as can be seen, incurable without some form of collective ownership. The capitalist system plays a great part in the causation of wars, while through its control of education and the Press it keeps large sections of opinion under the influence of ignorance and misinformation. These are among the evils which a new system must seem able to cure if it is to command our support. Some of these evils might be cured by any form of Socialism; but there are others which State Socialism would almost certainly not cure.

Power, securely held and long possessed, has nearly always a very bad effect on character, and makes the holders of power incapable of giving effect to the wishes of the democracy. The resulting evils are by no means least in a strong bureaucracy, such as State Socialism would establish. If the holders of executive power are to be amenable to the popular will, they must be in very direct touch with those whom their decisions affect, they must be easily removable, and they must be under the necessity of publicly defending the measures they adopt. If the present money-making incentive of the capitalist is removed, there must be found some other form of self-interest, presumably that of success in the public esteem, to prevent those who control industry from succumbing to technical conservatism and a Chinese adherence to tradition. I believe this to be possible under Guild Socialism, but highly improbable under State Socialism. I believe also that the distribution of different kinds of power in the hands of different authorities will secure some of those advantages which eighteenth-century political philosophers sought in the theory of checks and balances.

A powerful argument in favour of autonomous guilds in industry may be derived from the theory of democracy. Democracy is not realized by conferring power on the majority of any casual group of human beings; it is realized only when the group fulfils certain conditions in relation to the function concerned. This is recognized in the case of nationality: no sane person contends that British dominion in Ireland is in accordance with democratic principle, although it is carried out in accordance with the will of Parliament. It is recognized even more effectually as regards religious bodies: the power of Parliament to decide the dogmas of the Church of England has become obsolete. The general principle is: any group, whether geographical or not, which has strongly-marked interests that do not greatly affect people outside the group, should be self-governing in regard to such interests. The principle of nationality is one instance of this; self-government in industry is another.

The vastness of modern States and the helplessness of individuals in the grip of enormous organizations has an effect in diminishing responsible and vigorous initiative. Great organizations are an inevitable effect of industrialism; and industrialism will remain under any possible system, it is the strongest thing in the modern social world. But constructiveness and the creative spirit are essential to a healthy life in all who are naturally energetic. Unless men are to become apathetic and disillusioned, unless society is to become stereotyped and unprogressive, it must be possible for the more active-minded members of the community to feel that they are capable, by their actions, of effecting some improvement in the matters that interest them. At present, in industry, constructiveness finds no outlet except in the few great capitalists. It is difficult to believe that any system short of self-government could remedy this evil. The Syndicalists deserve credit for having first sought a cure, but their proposals are open to the objections that may be urged against anarchism, and also to the objection that no adequate provision is made for those political questions that are not primarily industrial. Peace and war, education, sanitation, and so on, are essentially geographical questions, and demand a geographical public authority. For this reason, the co-existence of the geographical State and the industrial Guild Congress seems to me to effect the necessary compromise between State Socialism and Syndicalism.

To sum up: the present system of private capitalism is to be condemned on account of its cruelty, rapacity and oppression, its tendency to promote wars, its hostility to enlightenment, and its extreme restriction of personal initiative. State Socialism is to be feared because, though it might cure poverty and secure economic justice, it would probably soon become rigid and Byzantine, even more hostile to initiative than the present system, and probably as favourable to misinformation as even the capitalist Press. Anarchism, which aims at avoiding these evils, would place no obstacles in the way of brigandage, and would probably soon end in a military tyranny. If the dangers of anarchism are to be avoided, and the evils of the existing system are to be remedied, Guild Socialism seems to me the plan which involves least of the evils to be feared under State Socialism. I believe that it is capable, not only of putting an end to poverty and economic injustice, but of securing the greatest sum of liberty and initiative that is possible to human nature at its present stage of development.

scottish left review

Since 2000 the Scottish Left Review has been Scotland's leading journal of radical politics. It is non-party but aims to provide a space for ideas and debate for those on the Left of all parties and none.

Read current issues and subscribe at

www.scottishleftreview.org

Reviews

Master Works

Vasily Grossman, *Everything Flows*, Harvill Secker, 290 pages, ISBN 9781846552366, £16.99
Andrey Platonov, *The Foundation Pit*, New York Review of Books, 224 pages, ISBN 9781590173053, $14.95

Two master works have now appeared in harness. Andrey Platonov was born in 1899, a railwayman's son. He started work at thirteen, and became an engine driver's assistant. The Revolution encouraged his talents, and he started publishing poems and articles in 1918, whilst studying engineering. During the twenties he became an expert in land reclamation, draining swamps and digging wells. He also built three small power stations. But he never stopped writing.

During the thirties, he was compelled to eat some of those words. He recanted several times, but he continued writing. His stories were only a little bit more acceptable to the authorities than before. His son was sent to the Gulag in 1938, contracted TB and died of it when he was released in 1941. Andrey was given a job on the Red Army's *Red Star* journal, working as a war correspondent on the recommendation of his friend, Vasily Grossman.

Vasily Grossman is by now already well known for his titanic novel, *Life and Fate*. We have been waiting for a long time for an accessible edition of *Everything Flows*, which now appears simultaneously in a NYRB edition in the United States and here under the flag of Harvill Secker. It was published before, under the title *Forever Flowing*, in a version by T. F.Whitney.

Both these books are now translated by Robert and Elizabeth Chandler, in an exceptional labour of love. They are beautifully written, even though they come from an unfinished work, still far from complete.

In an immortal tribute of vice to virtue the late Mr. Suslov, the apparatchik's apparatchik, said that *Life and Fate* had no chance of being published for at least two hundred years. This shows that Suslov had an exaggerated idea of the durability of his regime: but interestingly it also shows that he had sufficient taste and intelligence to understand that this masterpiece would indeed be read two hundred years after we have all gone.

If Suslov could utter such opinions about *Life and Fate*, he would nonetheless have had a heart attack about *Everything Flows*. Here, Grossman honours his murdered mother, to whom *Life and Fate* had been dedicated. He sets down a fictional version of her searing recollections of the great famine, of which she was a witness. It resulted from the forced collectivisation, and sent all Russia, and its Communist Party, into a convulsive turmoil. Out of it were to arise the purges, the trials, and the darkest pre-war years of the Soviet Union. Then followed the calamity of the Nazi invasion. Grossman's mother had subsequently been killed by the Gestapo because she refused to leave Ukraine when her son urgently pressed her to move away from the war to live with his family in Moscow, which might have offered her a marginally safer refuge. Grossman himself was sent off as a war correspondent to Stalingrad, so he was to become no stranger to the horrors of the Nazi invasion. But he always felt that his mother might have survived had he been more insistent on the need for her to uproot, and that is why he felt a towering debt to the woman commemorated in these two extraordinary works, and why he needed to record her memories of that terrible hunger.

Chapters 12 and 13 of *Everything Flows* take us into the camps. As Grossman says:

> 'A lot can be forgiven anyone who, amid the filth and stench of camp violence, remains a human being.'

Masha, who has endured sufficient anguish and despair, finally realised that the husband of whom she continually dreamed had already been shot, whilst her orphaned daughter was still lost in the great wastes of the Union of Soviet Socialist Republics

> 'and she was left without hope, entirely alone ... never would she see Yulia – neither today nor in future, when she was an old woman with grey hair. Lord, Lord, have pity on her. Pity her, Lord. Have mercy upon her. A year later she left the camp. Before returning to freedom, she lay for a while on some pine planks in a freezing hut. No one tried to hurry her out to work, and no one abused her. The medical orderlies placed Masha Lyubimova in a rectangular box made from boards that the timber inspectors had rejected for any other use. This was the last time anyone looked at her face. On it was a sweet, childish expression of delight and confusion ...'

Chandler adds a note to his translation, which says:

> 'These events are so tragic and so vast that they can seem entirely beyond understanding. Even Stalin's great purges of 1934-8 are easier to understand; they were, among other things, a successful attempt on Stalin's part to destroy,

or terrify into submission any members of the Soviet élite who might conceivably oppose him. It is harder to understand why a ruler should choose to destroy a huge part of the peasantry that had, until then, produced much of the nation's wealth.'

Chandler's incomprehension is shared by a number of other commentators, who offer different explanations in answering. Grossman's own explanations will not satisfy all the historians. But none will fail to recognise the human consequences of these terrible decisions, wrung out here by Grossman in tears of blood.

Platonov, too, was deeply affected by the famine, which shaped his thinking in *The Foundation Pit*. In this story, people are toiling to excavate a pit in which will be built an enormous structure, large enough to house all the people who live in a small town. They have ceased farming, and neither plough the fields nor sow any crops. There is nothing to eat, but the people dedicate themselves completely to the dream which they have of a radiant future that is due to arrive. Those who own anything are exiled, despatched down the river on a raft to the cold sea. Those who stay behind to dig gradually die of starvation.

Platonov had seen the forced collectivisation for himself. His work had taken him to the country, and in the villages he had seen all the horrors. Robert Chandler and Olga Meerson, in an afterword to the novel, suggest that Platonov had provided much of the testimony which convinced Grossman that he should compose *Everything Flows*. Be that as it may, these two writers are unique in Soviet literature, in the accuracy of their account of wholesale collectivisation, and the resultant famine. Others have written about these events, sometimes honestly and sometimes even courageously. But these two rise above the horrors they describe, to give us a powerful legacy. It is all the more extraordinary that these were such modest and retiring men.

Tatyana Tolstaya records a youthful utterance of Platonov:

> 'I know that I am one of the most insignificant of people. You have no doubt noticed this, but I also know another thing: the more insignificant a creature is, the more glad it is for life, because it is least deserving of it.'

Tolstaya continues:

> 'And further, the mysterious words: "for you being a man is just a habit – for me it is joy, a holiday ..."'

Such horrors. Such joys. Such an extraordinary people.

Ken Coates

The Tolstoys

Sophia Tolstoy, *The Diaries of Sophia Tolstoy*, translated by Cathy Porter with a foreword by Doris Lessing, Alma Books, 450 pages, hardback ISBN 9781846880803, £20

Sophia Behrs was only 18 when she was introduced to the 34-year-old Count Leo Tolstoy, in 1862, and by September of that year they were married in Moscow. On the eve of their wedding, Tolstoy asked his bride-to-be to read his diaries, in which he describes his sexual relationships with serfs, a love affair with one young woman in particular who bore him a child, and his homosexual leanings. The young Sophia was devastated and disgusted by what she had read:

> 'The whole of my husband's past is so ghastly that I don't think I shall ever be able to accept it ... When he kisses me, I am always thinking, "I am not the first woman he has loved". It hurts me so much that my love for him – the dearest thing in the world to me ... should not be enough for him.'

From this difficult beginning sprang a tortuous and tumultuous life together. The Tolstoys lived in Yasnaya Polyana, Leo's 4,000 acre estate, and had 13 children in all, eight of whom survived. Sophia was to be in charge of the estate, the children and Leo himself, and it is through her diary that we gain an insight into how unhappy she was with her lot. In 1863, after only a year of marriage, she writes:

> 'I am to gratify his pleasure and nurse his child, I am a piece of household furniture, I am a woman. I try to suppress all human feelings.'

Their relationship was composed of two disparate characters. Sophia wanted a more spiritual side to their life together, whilst Leo demanded sexual relations, but refused to use birth control. When Sophia did get pregnant he would become repulsed by her:

> 'My pregnancy is to blame for everything – I'm in an unbearable state, physically and mentally ... As far as Lyova is concerned I don't exist.'

From her diary the reader soon discovers that Sophia did everything within their relationship, around the estate, and was even a literary agent for her husband. She ensured copyright for his works and battled continuously with the Russian censors on his behalf. She put a tremendous amount of effort into advancing his writings, and every evening she would copy out his untidy drafts in her neat handwriting, returning them to Tolstoy the next day for him to revise once again, which would lead to still more copying for her. Sophia copied out *War and Peace* seven times! But it is this aspect of their relationship that provides her with a sense of being wanted and needed by her husband.

When he reached middle age Tolstoy turned away from writing towards shaping his own version of Christianity. In the mid-1880s, he became a religious guru and turned his back on fiction and on his wife. He threatened to give away all his property and the copyright to his works to the Russian people. Around this time Sophia's diary becomes more fraught:

> 'What I have predicted has come true: my passionate husband has died, and since he was never a friend to me, how could he be one to me now? This is not the life for me.'

On many occasions throughout the diary, the reader is privy to Sophia's longing to have the time to become a musician or artist:

> '... hundreds of times I have felt my intellectual energy stir within me, and all sorts of desires – for education, a love of music and the arts ...' But this was not to be: '... time and time again I have crushed and smothered these longings'.

She does have music lessons and tries, in a two-and-a-half hour session, to master the '8th Invention by Bach'. Her creative abilities were not only musical, for some of Sophia's fascinating photographs of the Tolstoy family are reproduced here.

The Diaries of Sophia Tolstoy is a 450-page tome spanning 57 years in the life of this remarkably intelligent and tolerant woman. Her life was not easy, for she loved her husband even though he tormented her and, in the background, they lived through some of the more turbulent times in Russian history. These private diaries offer the reader an insight into the predicament of women in the past (I can't see many 21st century females putting up with that kind of behaviour), but the pages are mainly filled with deep-seated neurosis, pain and anguish. They are not an easy read, so I would recommend a 'dipping-in-and-out' approach.

Abi Rhodes

A Q Khan

Gordon Corera, *Shopping for Bombs: Nuclear Proliferation, Global Insecurity and the Rise and Fall of the A.Q.Khan Network*, Oxford University Press, 304 pages, paperback ISBN 9780195375237, £12.99

The threatening face of the Pakistan scientist A.Q.Khan, which peers out banefully from the front cover of this book, sets the tone for what is inside.

Khan was, and perhaps still is, a major threat to the security of our world. That is not how he started out in life. As a young scientist he learnt his nuclear trade in The Netherlands, where he seems to have had almost unlimited access to what ought to have been most secret data about reprocessing and the essential centrifruges.

A photograph in the book of a Pakistani general surrendering shows the moment when Khan's national nuclear missionary zeal began. As a Pakistani, he felt deeply humiliated when Pakistan had to surrender to India in 1971, and lost a large part of its territory to what became Bangladesh. The young Khan would, from then on, do all he could to give his country a weapon which would, as he thought, make such a future surrender impossible.

Nationalism was the driving force that moved him. His attitude was rather like that of our own Ernest Bevin who, generations earlier, demanded his nuclear bomb with ' a bloody Union Jack on top'. That was also the conviction of the political leaders in Pakistan.Their bomb project began secretly, but it was well funded and staffed. Khan had whatever he wanted to bring the project to a successful conclusion. The secrecy was padded out with lies. Benazir Bhutto, in 1989, told a joint session of the US Congress that 'we do not possess nor do we intend to make a nuclear device. That is our policy.'

Perhaps it was hers. It was not the policy of those who held the levers of funding and power.

'All Praise to Allah' said the scientist who pushed the button in May 1998 and set off Pakistan's first nuclear explosion. If Khan's career had ended there, then it would have been bad enough that there had been a major breach of the Nuclear Non-Proliferation Treaty: another country added to the list of nuclear weapon states. But it did not end there. Khan became a model of active commercial free enterprise. He built up a vast international network, which supplied components and designs to anyone who wanted to buy. Primarily, his customers were Iran, North Korea and Libya.

I cannot believe for a moment, granted the interest shown in his activities by several surveillance organisations, not least the CIA, that his numerous trips abroad and the reasons for them were not well known to the authorities in his own country. The power of these organisations is even greater than I thought. When they wanted to inspect a cargo ship on its way to Libya, they simply ordered it to redirect to an Italian port where it was inspected and its cargo of nuclear components confiscated.

How the net was finally pulled in on Khan, the biggest fish in nuclear proliferation, makes this a scientific mystery story which is well told. In 2001, General Musharraf, dealing carefully with one who had become a national hero, put Khan under what amounted to house arrest. It was all done with great dignity. A retirement banquet in Khan's honour was held, and a special new post was created. Khan's days as an exporter were over. At least I like to think so, but it is optimistic to think that his entire global empire simply unravelled.

This is very much a 'proliferation is the big danger' book. The author, who works for the BBC as a security and terrorist expert, reflects the normal BBC perspective. Proliferation is the big worry. The nuclear arsenals of the major powers are probably going to be in place indefinitely and are not the major cause of concern. True, he does refer to Article VI of the Nuclear Non-Proliferation Treaty, which calls on nuclear weapon states to negotiate the elimination of their weapons, but that is not the focus of this book.

The Libyan story is worth a paragraph on its own. Gadaffi did not abandon his active nuclear weapons ambition, in 2003, because he was threatened or bombed. Indeed, Libya had been bombed once before, for other reasons, during Reagan's days. Gadaffi made an approach, first of all to the British, to tell them that, under certain conditions, he would give up his nuclear weapon efforts. But why? In his own words, this programme 'is not useful to Libya but it actually represents a danger and a threat to Libya's very integrity'. His Ambassador in London was even clearer. If we had nuclear weapons, 'we would be in more danger than if we didn't have them'.

What wisdom! The whole book is interesting and revealing, but these Libyan comments are amongst the best parts of it.

Bruce Kent

Iran

Mark Fitzpatrick, *The Iranian Nuclear Crisis: Avoiding Worst Case Outcomes,* Institute of Strategic Studies/Routledge (Adelphi Paper 398), 100 pages, paperback ISBN 978041546677, £15.99
Saira Khan, *Iran and Nuclear Weapons: Protracted Conflict and Proliferation,* Routledge, 168 pages, hardback ISBN 9780415453073, £75

The acquisition of nuclear weapons by Iran is a matter of deep concern – not only to western nuclear powers and their allies, but also to the international movement for nuclear disarmament. If the Islamic Republic of Iran develops the capacity to launch nuclear missiles against its enemies, this will not only seriously undermine the Nuclear Non-Proliferation Treaty (NPT) and encourage other countries to follow suit, it will increase the possibility of an outbreak of nuclear war.

Mark Fitzpatrick, in *The Iranian Nuclear Crisis*, analyses the problem from the point of view of the western powers. He produces the evidence that the intention of the Iranian authorities is to develop nuclear arms, and discusses past and possible future efforts to prevent such an eventuality.

Fitzpatrick completely dismisses the claims of Tehran that the aim is solely to enrich uranium for peaceful purposes. Legitimising the enrichment process would make it possible for an Iranian government to switch over to the production of nuclear weapons very speedily. It would also make it possible to manufacture them in secret, while claiming to be engaged on generating electricity for civilian purposes alone.

The introduction of sanctions, financial pressures, strict control of exports, and international vigilance are put forward as measures to be implemented to prevent Iran realising its nuclear ambitions. By isolating Iran and preventing it achieving economic prosperity, Fitzpatrick argues, not only will the development of nuclear weapons be obstructed, but also the support of the population for the Government and its policies will be undermined.

Fitzpatrick advocates, in addition, security assurances from the major powers to neighbouring states that Iran will not be permitted to intimidate them. Although he does not propose direct military intervention in Iran, he states that a deterrence strategy must include 'a credible threat of use of force if red lines are crossed' [p.84]. At the same time, he urges 'a corresponding reassurance to Iran's leaders that their country's sovereignty and security will not be threatened if "red lines" are observed'.

Saira Khan, in *Iran and Nuclear Weapons*, approaches the issue of Iran's nuclear ambitions from a very different standpoint. She argues that Iran's desire to develop nuclear weapons is fuelled by the protracted conflict with the United States.

In 1953, the USA intervened to secure the overthrow of Iran's Prime Minister, Mohammed Mossadeq and his government. It supported the Shah against popular opposition until he was overthrown. It failed to condemn Iraq for developing and using chemical weapons against Iran in the Iran/Iraq War. It failed to condemn Israel for bombing an Iraqi nuclear reactor in 1981. It launched the Gulf War against Iraq, and developed bases in Saudi Arabia. President George W. Bush labelled Iran as one of the 'axis of evil' states.

Saira Khan argues that protracted US hostility towards Iran has led Iran's leaders to conceive of a nuclear deterrent capability as a means of defending the country against some future military action directed at them. They have also come to regard the prestige attached to possession of nuclear weapons as essential to their aspiration to the role of a major power in the Gulf region. Furthermore, the United States has not objected to Israeli possession of nuclear weapons, nor to its failure to comply with the Nuclear Non-Proliferation Treaty. She comes to the conclusion that Iran will never give up its nuclear ambitions while it feels threatened by the US:

> 'As long as the US does not fashion a different style of foreign policy to Iran and terminate the protracted conflict with Tehran, it is unlikely for Iran to relinquish its nuclear programme.' [p.117]

Though democrats and progressives should have no illusions about the repressive nature of the Iranian regime, we should recognise that threats of military intervention – veiled or open – strengthen the Iranian authorities' case for seeking to develop nuclear weapons, and weaken internal opposition to it. While taking the strongest possible stand against Iran obtaining nuclear weapons, the idea of US, Israeli, or other western intervention in Iran must be totally condemned and opposed.

While repression and abuses of human rights in Iran should be strongly denounced, reforms and changes in the system are the business of the Iranian people. The sovereignty of Iran must be fully respected.

Both these books provide a great deal of background on Iran and its nuclear ambitions. Pressure, persuasion and sanctions may play a part in deterring or persuading Iran to abide by the Non-Proliferation Treaty, but threats of military intervention are counter-productive and should be totally ruled out.

Stan Newens

Gulag

Asim Qureshi, ***Rules of the Game: Detention, Deportation, Disappearance,*** **Hurst & Company, 234 pages, paperback ISBN 9781850659686, £12.99**

> 'What I'm trying to do here is, and this will be followed with the action in the next few weeks as I think you will see, is to send a clear signal out that the rules of the game have changed.'
>
> *Tony Blair, 5 August 2005*

Taking its cue from Tony Blair's candid remarks following the London bombings of 7 July 2005, Asim Qureshi's revealing and valuable book spells out how those changes impact on individuals around the world. Indeed, the impact pre-dated the tense summer of 2005, and began to be felt by people in different parts of the world very quickly in the days following the attacks on the United States in September 2001. In another memorable one-liner, Cofer Black, who was Director of the CIA's Counter-Terrorist Center, remarked that 'after 9/11 the gloves came off'. Qureshi's book examines some of the enduring consequences of the beating, bruising and worse that followed their removal.

Some of the first arrests were made in Bosnia. In particular, several Algerians who had come to Bosnia to fight with the Muslim community against the Serbs and Croats, were detained on 24/25 September 2001. Some of them had married Bosnian women, were settled in the country, and held Bosnian passports. Initially, the Bosnian authorities decided to release the men, but the United States insisted on their continued detention. Ultimately, they were given over into the custody of the Americans and wound up in Guantanamo, where they remained until release in 2009, when it was found they had no charges to answer.

In Britain, it was also Algerians as well as Libyans who were amongst the first to be targeted following 9/11. The haphazard nature of such detentions emerges all too plainly in the telling interviews conducted by the author, Moazzem Begg and their colleagues at Cageprisoners (www.cageprisoners.com), excerpts from which are reproduced here. This important organisation, with meagre resources but great dedication, tells us much about the war on terror and its impact on individuals, most of whom are completely innocent of any destructive or harmful intent.

In Pakistan, for example, detention was a money-spinner for officials. In 2005, one victim of this trade, Alam Ghafoor, told Cageprisoners:

> 'Over the previous four years, the Pakistani security services had kidnapped hundreds of foreign nationals on its streets, many of whom ended up in Guantanamo – it is claimed that 85 per cent of those who are detained at the base camp in Cuba were sold by the Pakistani government to the US at a price of $5,000 each.' P.27
> [Testimony of Alam Ghafoor to Cageprisoners, 11 August 2005]

Mr Ghafoor's testimony receives some measure of corroboration from no less a source than Pervez Musharraf, the former President of Pakistan, who wrote in his autobiography:

> 'Since shortly after 9/11 – when many Al Qaeda members fled Afghanistan and crossed the border into Pakistan – we have played multiple games of cat and mouse with them ... We have captured 672 and handed over 369 to the United States. We have earned bounties totalling millions of dollars ...' [quoted on p.137]

What of MI5's involvement in this global sweep? Ashraf Hossein was detained in Bangladesh between 1 December 2005 and 29 May 2008. He seems to have been caught up in the wake of the 7/7 bombings in London. He had travelled to Bangladesh to get married and also to visit his native town in Sylhet. A month after his marriage, he was arrested by the Bangladeshi authorities with, he thinks, two 'white men' wearing balaclavas in attendance. After a period of detention and abuse at the hands of his Pakistani captors, Mr Hossein met with two British officials, Liam and Andrew. His hopes that, as a British citizen, he would now find some 'justice, law and order' were quickly dashed:

> 'Liam says, "From our findings we see you are a highly trained individual aren't you, so why have you obtained all this training?" He then says, "Ahh so you are the mastermind for the atrocities in the UK, aren't you? So you know about the July 7 Bombings" saying this very calmly but with a sharpness coming from his throat.
>
> At that point I told Liam and Andrew, "it's not true, it's all been a mistake, I am innocent, I don't know why I am arrested, please tell me why I am here for, what have I done, please help me I am a British citizen." These guys have been abusing me for the last three weeks or so, beating me and threatening me that they will rape my wife. Whatever I have said or wrote is all made up; I did all this just to please the Colonel. The MI5 men just turned around and looked at the Colonel and shook their heads in disappointment. Liam said, "I think we need a break"...'

Mr Hossein was led away and beaten about his body, but 'not the face', on the instructions of the Colonel. On his return to the meeting room:

> 'Andrew says, "Are you okay, I hope you are okay and the break has done you some good." Liam says, "where were we, so you are a trained person from my notes I see you trained in Kashmir, bomb expert, I just agreed with him ..."'

Notwithstanding his 'confession', Mr Hossein was eventually released, although MI5 and the Bangladeshi security services continued to harass him and tried to buy his co-operation. It was many more months before he was able to return to Britain.

Rules of the Game contains much first-hand testimony to the folly of those who prosecute the 'war on terror'. But it is balanced by a measured assessment in the face of these depredations, which itself seems to reflect the enduring disposition of many of those whom the 'war on terror' has abused. In the author's own words:

> '... the purpose of this book is not to count numbers, it is to highlight the human value of what is taking place in the hope that those voices will appeal to the public and administrations to reverse the current trend.'

Tony Simpson

China in Africa

Deborah Brautigam, *The Dragon's Gift: The Real Story of China in Africa*, Oxford University Press, 398 pages, hardback ISBN 9780199550227, £18.99

Just over two years ago I reviewed four books on Africa in China, published in 2007. They all gave warnings of the possible threat of a new colonialism, this time not from European or American powers, but from China and, possibly, from India. But the conclusion was relatively hopeful, that China's approach to Africa was different, and that the more colonialist aspects were changing. Two years later, this book, by Deborah Brautigam, shows that there have indeed been changes for the better, and that Chinese policies were not so bad as some critics had assumed. Brautigam starts from Zhou Enlai's 'Eight Principles for China's Aid to Foreign Countries', announced in Ghana in 1964, which she prints in full in Appendix 1. These emphasised the principles of mutual benefit and equality, respect for sovereignty, and independent economic development. To this end, aid was to consist of low interest loans and provision of technical experts, who will have the same standards of living as local experts. Brautigam believes that these principles have largely been adhered to. Her evidence derives from her many visits, over a period of three decades, to projects in different parts of Africa, her discussions with Chinese officials both in Africa and in China, and rigorous research into relevant reports and other documentation.

Brautingam describes a number of joint projects involving both Chinese and African enterprises. These go back quite a long time – to the TanZam railway, starting in 1967 and completed ahead of schedule in 1975. From the 1970s onward, Chinese companies operating overseas were separated from their government ministries, and the banks financing them were required to work on commercial principles. By the 1990s, the authorities in Beijing were looking for 'value for money'. Competition, efficiency and 'market oriented' principles were required in the use of public money, including foreign aid.

Unlike most Western countries, China does not give cash aid, except for disasters and for technical and medical assistance. Joint projects between Chinese and African enterprises, which Brautigam has examined in person and in detail, are financed by what are called 'resource-backed loans'. These comprise, *inter alia*, infrastructure improvement, textile factories, and leather goods processing.

The scale of activity is impressive. Concessionary loans by China to Africa rose tenfold from the year 2000 to 2007 when they topped $1.7

billion. By that time, total financial flows from China to Africa were exceeding those of any other donors apart from the United States. Chinese loans by then even exceeded those of the World Bank.

The spread of China's interest in Africa is very wide. In nearly all Sub-Saharan Africa's states China had, by 2006-7, entered into Economic and Technical Agreements. The only exceptions were Gambia, Malawi, and São Tomé and Príncipe. The reason for these exceptions was that these countries continued to recognise Taiwan as China. The existence of two 'Chinas' has been a long-standing cause of Beijing's hesitation in reaching agreements with African governments. Otherwise, there are no evident preferences in Beijing's choice of partners in Africa. It is not even the case, as is often suggested, that Beijing is only interested in 'resource-rich' countries. Even China's Foreign Aid Loan agreements are to be found equally in countries without rich resources, throughout East Africa, for example, and in Senegal, Côte d'Ivoire and Ghana. The 'resource-backed' loans are not necessarily based on exploitation of mineral resources.

Brautigam's last chapter (11), entitled 'Rogue Donor? Myths and Realities', summarises the various arguments that are adduced to support the case against China's 'Dragon's Gift'. The first is that China's interest is really about oil or, alternatively, copper, iron ore, timber, etc. It is certainly true that China's interest in oil in Angola and in Sudan has been very obvious, but it has been no greater than that of other countries with major oil interests, and we have seen that China's activities are just as evident in African countries without rich resources.

Another argument which stresses China's 'neo-colonialism' is that China is less concerned with human rights and democratic governance than other foreign powers in Africa. This takes a bit of believing, especially in relation to the prevalence of corruption. China has partnered Mauritius, South Africa and Botswana, among less corrupt regimes, as well as the most corrupt, such as Equatorial Guinea and the Democratic Republic of the Congo. But so have the Western powers. Sudan and Zimbabwe are the two cases most frequently cited in criticising China's policies of partnering unsavoury regimes. In fact, the World Bank and Western powers have not been above providing aid and even selling arms to dictators. Japan and India both get oil from Sudan, and the Russians have sold arms to Khartoum. Zimbabwe is a special case where the Western powers have imposed sanctions, but China has not.

Brautigam provides evidence that China's policies in Zimbabwe, as well as in Sudan, are changing. Beijing has shown that it is anxious to follow the lead of African organisations such as the African Union and the regional Southern African Development Community (SADC). This reveals the real weakness of Africa, that such organisations are quite weak. Africa remains divided up by colonial rule into over fifty individual states, with each of which China, like the one-time colonial powers, reaches separate agreements.

Finally, arguments against China's policies in Africa relate to unfair subsidies and low environmental and social standards, especially labour standards. Again, Chinese policies can be shown to be changing. In 2007, China's Eximbank signed a memorandum of understanding with the World Bank's International Finance Corporation on what are called 'Equator Principles', a voluntary set of social and environmental principles. The Chinese Government can see that its reputation is at stake. By far the biggest criticism of Chinese trade practices in Africa is that Chinese manufactures, based on cheap Chinese labour, are being sold everywhere in Africa, and driving African manufacturers out of business. In some places cheap Chinese labour is settling in Africa at the expense of Africans. Brautigam can show many examples of joint Sino-African projects which are advancing African skills, but the fact remains that Sino-African trade mainly consists of the export of Chinese manufactures to Africa in exchange for Chinese imports of raw materials from Africa. This is little different from the colonial trade and what has been continued by the ex-colonial powers after African liberation. It remains to be said again that only all-Africa co-operative actions to resist this pattern of trade will bring any change.

Michael Barratt Brown

Capitalism

Fred Magdoff and Michael D. Yates, *The ABCs of the Economic Crisis: What Working People Need to Know,* **Monthly Review Press, 144 pages, paperback ISBN 9781583671955, £9.95**

Richard D. Wolff, *Capitalism Hits the Fan: The Global Economic Meltdown and What to Do About It,* **Olive Branch Press, 262 pages, paperback ISBN 9781566567848, £16.99**

Alan S. Kahan, *Mind versus Money: The War between Intellectuals and Capitalism,* **Transactions Publishers, 312 pages, hardback ISBN 9781412810630, £29.95**

Three books in very different styles which complement each other. The financial crisis has prompted two of them. The third is a thorough examination of the roots of capitalism and why intellectuals both support and criticize it.

My main observation concerns a confusion between capitalism and market. The two are not the same. I go to my local farmers' market. Are they capitalists? Capitalism is a particular structure of production, albeit with differences between countries. There have been many commentaries about this.

ABCs of the Economic Crisis takes us back to the seminal work of Baran and Sweezy (1966). It is an important introduction to the chaotic world of capitalism. It contains all the definitions we need to know and handles hedge funds, futures, leveraged buyouts, structured investment vehicles, and subprime loans with ease. The chapter 'How Did It Happen' is an excellent exposition and translation of technical obfuscation for readers.

It is summed up by the photo on the front cover of a cowboy-looking police officer presiding over the eviction of a woman holding her children's toys. The book makes scathing and startling comments about the connections between macro-economics and the personal implications. It should be on students' reading lists.

Capitalism Hits the Fan takes us through a series of articles written by the author since 2005, many of them prescient. It delves into some of the definitions of neo-cons and what they were after. I loved the piece about 'Nominating Palin Makes Sense', charting what has happened to the Republicans, and to the Democrats. It is an interesting reflection on the subject matter of all three books about capitalism. We should not forget the role of political parties. The three books combine economic, political and religious analysis in a fascinating way.

Then we come to Kahan's book. This is well researched and worth anybody's money, so to speak. Dismissive of Karl Marx, 'over-simplifier', (p.137), but he explained the world with tremendous force (p 138), followed by an excellent analysis of money and its dehumanization, and the implications of anti-semitism by anti-capitalist intellectuals. This is the most interesting chapter:

> 'The German socialist leader August Bebel … remarked that "anti-semitism is the socialism of fools". The point is not to convict Marx or Marxists of anti-semitism. It is to show how anti-semitism could gain strength from anti-capitalist ideas and become an episode in the struggle of mind versus money.'

The problem is surely that one could apply this to anti-Marxism with its anti-semitic undertones. As a result 'mind versus money' loses its force.

The quotes in this book are legion. References to Rousseau,

Montesquieu, Hume, Hirschman, Smith, Simmel, Tocqueville, Socrates and many more make you realize what a rich world of the 'mind' exists. A classic one, I paraphrase, 'preachers produce violence, merchants produce peace' (p.79). Making money was a more innocent occupation than religion. It civilized the aggression of religion.

An interesting thesis. Even the reference to Mozart, 'The Magic Flute', which extols the value of work, is a valuable insight into the history of capitalism and how the ideas appeared in the librettos of cultural heroes. It shows us how hegemonic ideas penetrate everything, even 'shopping' (p. 79).

Chapters on the 'Honeymoon between Intellectuals and Capitalism', then 'Why the Honeymoon Ended' are clever disguises for intellectual analysis. This is a very interesting book.

The three are an important addition to the literature on the puzzling subject of capitalism, why it persists, how it destroys things, and why nothing is done about it.

Richard Minns

Socialism

Leo Panitch, *Renewing Socialism – Transforming Democracy, Strategy and the Imagination*, Merlin Press, 226 pages, paperback ISBN 9780850365917, £14.95

Recently interviewed on Canadian television, the author was asked why he didn't join the Canadian New Democratic Party (NDP): he replied that he had been looking for a party to join all his life, so far without success. This book of essays presumably suggests what the parameters of such a party might look like. The text is largely made up of articles written for *Socialist Register* (of which the author is a joint editor with Colin Leys) before the present ongoing financial crisis.

In the first chapter, however, Panitch warns us presciently that capitalist crisis is an organic phenomenon integral to the capitalist system itself, enabling it to resolve its present contradictions and preparing the ground, if necessary, to move to a new operational mode. For socialists these crises provide both opportunities and dangers and too often we have found it difficult to take advantage of the opportunities. This is the case both for social democratic and communist parties, and Panitch believes that this was partly because they were building the wrong kind of parties. This brings us to the central thrust of the book: that we require new, or transformed existing parties, to galvanise into action a mass working-class movement committed to a socialist outcome. The New Left of the 1960s pinned its hopes on the rise of democratic socialism advancing in both the East and West, conjoining with Third World struggles for colonial liberation. What transpired was not revolution but counter-revolution with the neutering of trade unions, the adoption to one degree or another by social democratic parties of the neo-liberal agenda, the collapse of the Soviet bloc, and economically brutal capitalist restoration. At the same time, successful colonial liberation in the Third World became blighted by under-development and repressive factionalism, all exacerbated by Western intervention, both armed and economic. No wonder many socialists and radicals prefer involvement, if at all, in single issue campaigns and social movements rather than the messianic world view of yesteryear. This is at a time when many of the major fault lines of globalised capitalism are taking on an immediacy likely to threaten life on the planet itself. How can a mass socialist movement be resuscitated to begin to tackle these problems? For the writer a first step is the re-examination of both the successes and failures of the international labour movement, but as Panitch, quoting Marx, makes clear, 'finding once more the spirit of revolution, not making its ghost walk about again'.

In the main, Panitch looks to Lukács and Gramsci for his model of the mass party, which should not be primarily about 'putting forward a team of political leaders' at election time. Nor is it 'that of forging a small band of revolutionaries', it is the shaping of an 'economic group – and turning them into qualified political intellectuals, leaders and organisers'. The last quotation is from Gramsci's *Prison Notebooks,* and Panitch expands and develops the idea of class identity in a contemporary setting.

In chapter two, 'Observations on Communism's Demise', the author draws upon a 1990 visit to vehicle assembly plants in the Soviet Union at the height of Gorbachev's reforms. He describes in some detail the malaise affecting the workforce and its seeming imperviousness to reforms from the top. For Panitch this was partly owing to the reforms' implicitly contradictory nature, granting a degree of industrial democracy but also endorsing the tyrannies associated with capitalist market forces. The workers used their new freedoms to slacken the work pace, which Panitch noted was much harder than that of their Western counterparts.

The text moves on to discuss the work of C.B. Macpherson, a prominent Canadian academic, who through a lifetime of intellectual activity sought to assemble a synthesis of the 'insights' of Marxism and the 'valuable parts of the liberal tradition'. This is a dense but interesting chapter with Panitch drawing on Macpherson's work to take issue with the criticism of Ellen Wood. Panitch uses the opportunity to discuss democracy and the state in an incipient socialist state. Such a state would quickly be assailed by hostile powers and he realises the need for internal defensive coercion and the resulting danger of generalised repression.

The legacy of the *Communist Manifesto* forms the backdrop to the next essay, and Panitch situates the text as the inspirational foundation stone in the development of the mass organisations of the working class, the trade unions and the social democratic parties. For him we have now arrived at a situation where organised communism is largely eclipsed, and social democracy has mostly abandoned any pretence of socialist aims, joining with the power élite in worshipping at the altar of the market. It is therefore ironic that the contemporary period has seen Marx's predictions about the nature and scope of capitalism realised, albeit a little later than he imagined. We now have a truly globalised economy, but unfortunately many would agree that as Perry Anderson has remarked, 'no collective agency able to match the power of capital is yet on the horizon'. In this context Panitch accepts that the New Left has failed to transform the existing social democratic and communist parties, but considers we should return to the *Manifesto* to put back on the agenda the irreconcilability of democracy with capitalist property relations as a key ideological concept. As Marx put it, 'the free development of each is the condition for the free development of all'.

In the chapter 'Bringing Class Back In: Reflections on a Strategy for Labour', Panitch discusses the relationships of trade unions and social movements in the context of their feminisation, together with the changed workplace situation under the neo-liberal dispensation, linking it with the changes in the composition of the working class. Stressing the centrality of trade unions both in the industrial and political arenas, Panitch appeals for strategies that are ambitious rather than always defensive, and that make radical demands on the state. At the same time, unions should adopt an educationally transforming strategy for members to root out residual racism, sexism, homophobia and anti-environmentalism amongst the membership.

The book is meant to inspire weary socialists and it certainly does make a bold attempt, with the final chapter and interview addressing the problem of pessimism on the Left directly. Additionally, apart from the many ideas and insights contained within the text, Panitch thinks that socialism has always been inspired by an element of utopian thinking. He therefore suggests the resuscitation of utopian thinkers of an earlier period with the assistance of the socialist philosopher Ernst Bloch. Bloch was convinced that, 'unconditional pessimism therefore promotes the business of reaction', and he very well might have a point.

This is a thoughtful book, if not a succinct whole. It is an amalgam of separate articles, and leaves the reader feeling that a more structured explanation of Panitch's ideas would be welcome. It will, however, reward the reader with its perspicacity, knowledge and stimulating ideas. The intellectual vigour of Panitch's thinking, and his abandonment of old shibboleths, is to be praised and emulated.

John Daniels

What Price European Union?

Perry Anderson, *The New Old World*, 564 pages, Verso, hardback ISBN 9781844673124, £24.99

Verso for New Left Books has published in one large volume twelve of Perry Anderson's essays contributed to the *London Review of Books* between 1996 and 2008, plus an essay in *New Left Review* of May-June 2009. The result comprises 547 pages of text and a 17 page index. The title and the painting of Narcissus on the cover are designed to suggest a dream of a new Europe reflecting the virtues of an older Europe. The index tells us something about the nature of the essays. It is an index of names, not of subjects. Each essay is a massive review of the literature on the subjects of the book – the development of the European Union, its largest members – Germany, France and Italy – and two of the Union's major problem areas – a divided Cyprus and a not yet admitted Turkey. The position of the United Kingdom is not discussed. The literature reviewed is largely from writers in the United States. European writers, as the author explains, having been responsible for masses of descriptive work, have not been concerned with theorising, with the exception of Alan Milward, to whom the book is dedicated. It is an interesting fact that there are no references to the writings either of the leading Member of the European Parliament, Ken Coates, or of Jacque Delors's economic adviser, Stuart Holland, one-time British MP and adviser to the Portuguese President. Their absence leaves not only a hole in the literature reviewed, but also a hole in the European Union story. By involving the churches as well as the unions in the social argument, Ken Coates won the support of pretty well the whole European Parliament for the Delors proposals with wide popular support, but not with that of the Governments, which had begun to follow Reagan and Thatcher into neo-liberal globalism.

What can we learn, then, from this great tome? In discussing 'Origins and Outcomes', Perry Anderson identifies the great gap that has opened up between the dream of a federal Europe, with external political and internal social responsibilities, such as the founding genius, Jean Monnet, once envisaged, and writers such as Jurgen Habermas have espoused, and the reality. What has emerged has been essentially a free trade area – a Common Market – with no more than nominal common responsibilities, where the separate nation states each retain their individual, unlimited sovereignty. Even the rather limited attempts to achieve a federal constitution with a President and some common internal and external policies were rejected in referenda by France and The Netherlands, and a modified 'Lisbon Treaty' that followed was rejected also by the only country carrying out a referendum on this Treaty, Ireland, though Ireland was one of the main beneficiaries of European subsidies The reason for these rejections, the author insists, derives from the ending of moves by Jacques Delors and others towards any form of Social Europe, and the adoption of neo-liberal policies of free markets, resulting in a wholly unequal impact of the Union on a small class of big businessmen and financiers and a governing élite, on the one hand, and, on the other, the mass of the several populations, especially the young, the women and the poor, but increasingly also some middle classes whose social services have been cut.

The three long chapters in the book, respectively on Germany, France and Italy, trace a long process of disintegration of any original commitment to a federal European Union, even as a guarantee of the ending of the appallingly destructive nature of the European wars of the Twentieth Century. Germany was able to unify its Western and Eastern parts within the Union, and rather shakily re-establish its capital in Berlin, with a German at the head of a highly restrictive European Central Bank. France abandoned most of de Gaulle's independent positions. Italy lost its Socialist commitment in the embrace of Berlusconi. More surprisingly, all three became enamoured of the NATO alliance and its American leadership, even eventually supporting United States military aggression. United States governments had promoted European Union as a counterweight to Soviet Communism, but with the ending of the Cold War still saw the containment of Russia as a major policy objective. From this arose US interest in a base in Cyprus, in the entry of Turkey's military strength not only into NATO, but also into the European Union, and, ultimately, also of Ukraine. Anderson's chapters on Cyprus and on Turkey reveal the British policy of divide and conquer between the Greek and Turkish parts of the island, and the desire to use Turkey as a moderate

Moslem ally in containing Russian ambitions in the Near East.

Within this world picture, Anderson raises the interesting question of what had made for Europe's economic, military and cultural world dominance over at least five hundred years. The answer he gives draws from those writers (he quotes François Guizot and Edgar Morin) who saw the very diversity and competitive antagonisms of the European powers, not just military, but ideological – Classical, Jewish and Christian – as the source of Europe's pre-eminent development. With much reduced intra-European competition today and, indeed, with the European Union's subservience to the United States, development might be expected to come from US-Chinese or Indian competition. The threat of terrorism and the migration to Europe of many millions of Muslims is considered in this context, but this is not seen as a stimulus to development, rather as a hangover from colonialism; Muslim immigrants, though often resistant, even rebellious, showing no multi-cultural, multi-confessional, competitive spirit. The class struggles in Europe that emerged in the mid-Twentieth century had died down by the Twenty First; even Social Democratic votes in Scandinavia, let alone in the United Kingdom, Germany or The Netherlands, dropping to 20% or below. So Perry Anderson ends the book with an equivocal question about European dynamic disequilibrium. 'In due course', he concludes,

> 'a prolonged economic recession might re-ignite the engines of political conflict and ideological division that gave the continent its impetus in the past. So far, in today's Europe, there is little sign of either. But it remains unlikely that time and contradiction have come to a halt.'

Since Anderson's last writings, the financial crisis in Greece and similar problems of debt in Spain and Portugal, and German resistance to bailing them out, have put the whole future of the Union into question.

Perry Anderson's essays are full of interesting information and imaginative questions, but the book is hard to read, not only because of its great length, its many references and convoluted sentences, but also because of his use of French, German and Italian words, and even of English words whose meaning is not clear. Just three examples of the latter which I baulked at were 'conflictuality', 'catalaxy' and 'decathexis', but there were others which may be in common use in American academia, where the author now resides, but do not appear in standard dictionaries. We have learnt so much from his writings in the past that is a pity that this book was not subjected to some friendly editing for the general reader.

Michael Barratt Brown

On the Broo

Christopher Harvie, *Broonland: The Last Days of Gordon Brown*, Verso, 224 pages, paperback ISBN 9781844674398, £8.99

Fiddled statistics on employment and public debt, catastrophic distance-learning projects, ditto for computerisation schemes, raids on pensions funds, selling off gold cheap, mud-wrestling with Tony Blair, yet bankrolling his delusions. Taxes that are baffling but real; tax credits that are baffling but illusory. Programmes to cut public sector jobs; programmes promising more public sector jobs. Transport, higher education, public culture: all kept anorexic. This is before we get to the motor itself, the property-and-retail/VAT fraud carousel which sucks in imports, piles up trade deficits, then attempts to correct these by 'inward investment', a euphemism for foreign takeovers and, less seductively, international hot money. Welcome to Broonland.

From these musings in *The Guardian's* 'Comment is Free' blog, Chris Harvie has expanded *Broonland* from blog to book. It is more a sort of biography, less the obsequious interviews of the official sort, and the confectionary of quotes from the unofficial sort. Written before the great leader's exit from Number 10, it almost charts Gordon Brown's trajectory back to earth, but I would defy any satirist to have the imagination to dream up the head in hands contrition over 'that bigoted woman'.

I have read two types of book by Chris Harvie, the heavy analytical academic, and the humorous commentary. *Broonland* is at times an uneasy compromise between the two. But with his subject moving from a self confident Calvinist and ambitious young politician to senior croupier at Blair's Downing Street casino, and the lack of quotable and attributable comments on Brown, the character has to be squeezed out of dry facts and statistics sometimes created by Gordon Brown and at other times created by the activities of his finally-to-be-worshipped free markets, which eventually surrounded and ambushed him.

For those who may think that Harvie is being harsh on Brown, I came across a copy of his speech (typed in caps as is his wont) to the Scottish Labour Conference on 12th March 1995 in Inverness. As the applause greeted him, a banner was unfurled from the balcony calling for the retention of Clause 4, prompting Jack McConnell to creep up and down the aisles posing the question 'Who did that?' to likely culprits. Meanwhile, Brown, oblivious to this diversion, delivered this speech specially tailored for his Scottish audience:

'When they're planning to sell off our stations our
  Rail track
  Our trains
  Our bridges
  Even the Forth Railway Bridge
When 600 million pounds has been spent in city fees to donors of the Conservative Party
With John McGregor, the former transport minister who privatised rail, now standing as a director of a company advising on the sell off of British Rail
Let us be clear about the motivation of all those involved – in this the second great train robbery.
The only network they're interested in protecting is the old boys network
The only track they want to be travelling on is the inside track
The only connections they're interested in making are city connections
And the only train that really concerns them is ... the gravy train
Not service they're interested in ... but self service that's the Tory Party.
No longer a party of the whole nation – now exposed simply as a run-down branch of network south east
Let us be clear
It is not our trains that should be driven off the tracks – it is rail privatisation itself and we're going to keep the railways in public hands just as we stopped the VAT rise
It's time to call a halt to the privatisation hand outs
It's time to blow the whistle on the boardroom excesses of the great and the greedy.
It's time to call an end to the share option millions, the insider dealers, the dubious tax exiles
These people never needed to wait for the Saturday National Lottery Draw Every day of the week they've been been awarding themselves all the biggest prizes on offer
It's not a National Lottery.
It's a National disgace and we'll stop it.
Because it is wrong that one hundred and ten million pounds of privatisation share options are given tax privilege while middle and lower income families are taxed more to receive less
We will end the tax privilege and use the money to help the many not the few
Because it is wrong that telephone number salaries are paid to executives
When BT added ones to their telephone numbers they didn't tell us they'd also added noughts to their salaries
We will give the privatisation regulators power to cut prices for millions of consumers where there is abuse and so redistribute resources from these powerful interests to ordinary people in this country
Because it is wrong that unbridled speculation is threatening the livelihoods of thousands of men and women ...

Wrong that a bank can virtually become a betting shop
Wrong that some bankers are more obsessed about their bonuses than the jobs and savings of those affected by their bankruptcy ...'

Chris Harvie's *Broonland* relates the actual onward route march of Gordon Brown from Inverness, through the bonfire of the pledges in 1996 and his irresistible rise to the top of the Labour Party. A Labour Party which was reduced to fighting the recent election that lead to Brown's dénouement with the old policy-free slogan 'If you vote SNP you'll let the Tories in – Only Labour can beat the Tories!'

Chris Harvie will not miss the irony of English voters sending Brown homewards to think again, this time with further empirical evidence to ponder that, if Scotland votes Labour to keep the Tories out, and England votes Tory, you get a Tory government. Will the old slogan work the next time and put the frighteners on the Scottish electorate as before, or will the electorate get fed up that Labour just does not deliver. Adding to the electoral evidence on Labour's inability to deliver is *Broonland,* which lays bare the collapse of the faux ideology that the left can manage capitalism to produce fair outcomes. I'm afraid that vulgar wealth at one end of the axis and grinding poverty at the other are both prerequisites of a capitalist society, and the outcome of its theory being put into practice.

Henry McCubbin

Benn

Tony Benn, *Letters to my Grandchildren: Thoughts on the Future*, Hutchinson, 224 pages, hardback ISBN 9780091931261, £18.99, paperback ISBN 9780099539094, £8.99

Tony Benn has ten grandchildren, which might keep him busy enough as an adviser. Not all of us are as successful as he has been in motivating other people to do things which involve them in considerable efforts, and some of us, at any rate, have had sufficient cause to doubt whether their own advice, whether to children or grandchildren, might not be too assiduously received. But Tony Benn's most recent previous book was called *Dare to be a Daniel,* and he is once again living up to that instruction.

Here he sets out his opinions on civil disobedience, on nuclear war, and on non-alignment. Far from talking down to the grandchildren, he presents them with a serious argument. He also tries hard to set a serious example, of optimism and confidence in the possibilities contained in our futures.

He transmits the thoughts of American Presidents:

> 'I have seen war on land and sea. I have seen blood running from the wounded. I have seen men coughing out their gassed lungs. I have seen the dead in the mud, I have seen cities destroyed. I have seen 200 limping, exhausted men come out of line – the survivors of a regiment of a thousand that went forward 48 hours before. I have seen children starving. I have seen the agonies of mothers and wives. I hate war.'

So said President Franklin D. Roosevelt. Roosevelt was echoed by Dwight Eisenhower, 'himself a general'.

> 'Every gun that is made, every warship launched, every rocket fired signifies in the final sense a theft from those who hunger and are not fed, those who are cold and are not clothed. The world in arms is not spending money alone. It is spending the sweat of is laborers, the genius of its scientists, the hopes of its children … This is not a way of life at all, in any true sense. Under the cloud of threatening war, it is humanity hanging from a cross of iron.'

And yet, in spite of these warm words, more recent Presidents have given us the doctrine of full spectrum dominance, and the brutal wars in Iraq and Afghanistan.

That was how Benn entered his eighties as Chairman of the Stop the War Coalition. This was an affirmation, which it was entirely right to make.

But the future? Who knows? At a time of meltdown in human institutions, old verities become fluid, or have even evaporated. The Labour Party, to which Benn devoted his adult life, (and he began precociously) may indeed be part of the present meltdown. What will not melt down is the commitment which arises from the understanding that we are members of one another. Being members of one another, we learn, one from another. That is why it is fitting that Benn himself, 'living as I do "in a blaze of autumn sunshine"' can realise that 'I have learned more from my children and grandchildren than I did from my parents and therefore look with love and thankfulness on the human family'.

Perhaps the grandchildren will listen. But whether they do or not, there will be others who find this message acceptable.

Ken Coates

Later to Win?

David John Douglass, *The Wheel's Still in Spin*, published by Read 'n' Noir, an imprint of Christie Books of Hastings, East Sussex, distributed by Central Books Ltd, 99 Wallis Road, London E9 5LN. 466 pages with end notes, 120 photographs, a glossary and a list of organisations, paperback ISBN 139781873976364, £9.99

This second volume of autobiography by a Durham and Yorkshire miner and scholar was described by the publisher as part of a trilogy, 'Stardust and Coaldust'. The first volume, *Geordies – Wa Mental,* appeared in 2008, and my review appeared in *Spokesman 108*, on page 65. I apologise here for misspelling the author's surname then with a single 's'.

The volume reviewed here describes David Douglass's life in the decade 1969 – 1979. He was born in Tyneside in 1948. The title is taken from the Bob Dylan lyric *The Times They Are A-Changin'* quoted in the introduction.

And don't speak too soon
For the wheel's still in spin
And there's no tellin' who that it's namin'
For the loser now will be later to win
For the times they are a-changin'

The introduction, which has no named author, also refers to the Vietnam War and the worldwide revolutionary struggles that followed. The author's account places him in that struggle, and this volume, like the first, describes the social background of a politicised coal miner if not a typical one. The Vietnam War and the civil war in Northern Ireland must have influenced the author strongly. His perspectives moved through many associations from Young Communists through the 'Revolutionary Workers Party (Trotskyist) Doncaster Regional British Section Fourth International – Posadist' (the title of a home-made mineworkers style banner made with the help of his artistic wife Maureen) to being a member and organiser for Sinn Fein, an armed supporter of an expected revolutionary armed struggle, and an applicant for membership of the IRA.

It is no surprise to the reader that the stress of pit work and the intensity of his studies and political activities led to a serious nervous breakdown which a warm social life, sometimes lubricated by drugs, his love of music, and his impromptu singing of folksong at *céilithe* were unable to prevent. Sexual freedom didn't seem to work too well, either.

It is worth mentioning that among his early influences are two members of the Bertrand Russell Peace Foundation. Michael Barratt Brown was at Sheffield University's Extra Mural Department, where David Douglass was a day-release student of economics, political theory, social history, maths, statistics and English. The author also mentions our late and deeply mourned Ken Coates who was then opposing the sale of gunboats to Chile's General Pinochet.

The author's consistent commitment in these two volumes is to the ultimate and, as he saw it, inevitable success of the working class in a Marxist-socialist revolution. He was one of those working hard for it, even to the extent of organising military training of comrades with live ammunition on the moors of Northumberland. In this context his choice of Bob Dylan's verse as a title deserves examination. Who was losing in the 1970s, and who was seen then as later to win? In 1972 and in 1974, NUM strikes were successful, but only in restoring miners' earnings against rapid inflation. They were later to lose and lose heavily in 1984, and the author knew all about that in 2009 when this volume went to the printers. So did he choose Dylan's verse for the comfort of a promise of success yet to be delivered? And if he did, what will volume three have to say about the likely route of that success when the author has described the awful, premeditated attack on the labour movement, on democracy and on civil liberties that was 1984?

We will need more than a roulette wheel or even dialectical materialism to make the world sustainable for people, democracy, justice and peace. When we have overcome the distraction of the war on terror we will need some clear thinking about equity, differentials, resource depletion, carbon footprints, lifestyles, population, human rights and the better regulation of the military industrial complex.

Christopher Gifford